Sleep With Me

Hanif Kureishi was born and brought up in Kent. He read philosophy at King's College, London. In 1981 he won the George Devine Award for his play *Outskirts*, and in 1982 he was appointed Writer in Residence at the Royal Court Theatre. In 1984 he wrote *My Beautiful Laundrette*, which received an Oscar nomination for Best Screenplay. His second film, *Sammy and Rosie Get Laid*, was followed by *London Kills Me*, which he also directed. *The Buddha of Suburbia* won the Whitbread Prize for Best First Novel in 1990 and was made into a four-part drama series by the BBC in 1993. His version of Brecht's *Mother Courage* has been produced by the Royal Shakespeare Company and the Royal National Theatre. His second novel, *The Black Album*, was published in 1995. With Jon Savage he edited *The Faber Book of Pop* (1995). His first collection of short stories, *Love in a Blue Time*, was published in 1997. His story 'My Son the Fanatic', from that collection, was adapted for film and released in 1998. *Intimacy*, his third novel, was published in 1998.

HANIF KUREISHI

Sleep With Me

faber and faber
LONDON·NEW YORK

First published in 1999
by Faber and Faber Limited
3 Queen Square London WC1N 3AU
Published in the United States by Faber and Faber Inc,
a division of Farrar, Straus and Giroux Inc, New York

Typeset by Faber and Faber Ltd
Printed in England by Mackays of Chatham plc, Chatham, Kent

A CIP record for this book
is available from the British Library

ISBN 0-571-19796-5

2 4 6 8 10 9 7 5 3 1

For Monique

Characters

Stephen, 42
Charles, 50
Lorraine, 22
Julie, 37
Russell, 42
Sophie, 41
Barry, 53
Anna, 25

Late summer/early autumn 1997.

Sleep With Me was first performed at the Cottesloe Theatre, Royal National Theatre, London, on 14 April 1999 with the following cast:

Stephen Sean Chapman
Charles Jonathan Hyde
Julie Sian Thomas
Barry Peter Wight
Sophie Penny Downie
Lorraine Kacey Ainsworth
Russell Adrian Lukis
Anna Michelle Gomez

Director Anthony Page
Designer Tim Hatley
Lighting Designer Howard Harrison
Music Jason Carr
Sound Designer Christopher Shutt
Company Voice Work Patsy Rodenburg

Act One

SCENE ONE

The garden of a house in the English countryside.
  Stephen is outside working on a manuscript. On one side of him lies his friend Charles, asleep but stirring. On the other side is a shaded pram or buggy containing a baby.

Stephen How can you be so tired?

Charles It's been a long century.

He goes back to sleep.
  The baby starts to cry. Stephen puts toys in the buggy. Silence, before more crying. Then Stephen pushes it with one foot; silence again – for a moment.

Julie (*off*) Stephen . . . Stephen! People will be here soon . . . I'm cooking. There's a lot to do. Sean's got to be changed . . . Someone should tidy the sitting-room and the conservatory. Where's Lorraine? Lorraine!

Hearing his wife coming, Stephen starts to move away, leaving his dark glasses, pens, books, behind. Then he stops and watches her.
  Julie comes on from beside the house carrying flowers and herbs. She quietens and kisses the child.

Have you seen Stephen?

Charles shakes his head.

Sshh . . . sshh . . . my baby, my beautiful little fat-cheeked man, quiet, Mummy's here . . . it's still hot, I know . . . Mummy's got a few things to do – on her own, clearly. Have a nap for a long time . . . Daddy loves you, Mummy loves you . . . you're safe . . . everything's all right . . .

As she talks, she starts to look through Stephen's things: she opens his manuscript and examines it – until in the distance a voice is heard.

Barry (*off*) This way! Sophie!

Julie replaces the things, checks the child once again, and goes off, placing a flower on Stephen's manuscript.

Julie Stephen . . . Lorraine . . .

When she has gone, Stephen returns to his place. He puts the flower in his pocket and resumes work. Soon he hears nearer voices.

Barry (*off*) It's not far! Come on! Up the hill!

Stephen Charles –

Charles Finished? Can I read it?

Stephen I can hear other people.

Charles What?

Barry (*off*) It's over here! That was the gatehouse, not the place!

Charles I don't think we're ready for such excitement . . .

Stephen and Charles pick up Stephen's things and hurry off just as Sophie and Barry cycle on.

Barry The size of it. A cottage, you said.

Sophie I'm tired. It was far from the station. (*Pause.*) They're usually only here weekends and holidays. Julie said there's a river, and stables, barns and a tennis court. She said –

Barry No one actually lives here? The kids at school would love this. (*He notices the child in the buggy.*) We've come here to get away from that.

Sophie Look at little Sean . . . Hello. You're lovely. (*Pause.*) What do you think? So much hair . . .

Barry looks around. Sophie pulls a dress from her ruck-sack.

Barry They won't be dressed up will they? I'm not doing that.

Sophie I know.

Barry I wish I'd brought the tent. We could camp in the garden.

Sophie Perhaps we will sleep outside. And bathe in the river, and –

Barry I better fix the gears on the bike before we leave. I don't want to be late home tomorrow. There's that marking to do. You have to be enthusiastic for the first few days of the new term. (*He goes to the baby and replaces his toys.*) All right, all right.

Sophie lets down her hair, and combs it.

Just us for the first time in . . . I can't even remember. Children certainly stop you talking. Perhaps that's why people have them. (*He indicates the dress.*) When did you get it?

Sophie I went to the charity shop yesterday.

Barry It's been a long time since you've worn anything nice. I hope we have a good time, don't you?

Sophie Yes. You've cheered up. Look at this hem. Is it going to come down?

Barry No. No.

Sophie Yes it is.

Barry What does it matter?

3

Sophie It's the way everything is.

Barry I'm sweating. It's my heart. I'm at that age. I go to more hospitals than I do parties.

Sophie At least . . . did you remember the wine? Sorry.

Barry It cost enough.

Sophie We can't give them any rubbish.

Barry I'd sooner read Stephen's bank statements than his books. But it's other people's money they've got.

Sophie Julie's not rich, she works for a living. Stephen . . . After he won the Oscar and went to Hollywood everyone pursued him. He's spent the last three years standing behind his letter-box while they stuff money through it. But he's been trying to get back to his own work.

Barry That time . . . I thought he'd come to see you, as he does when I'm not there. How often is it?

Sophie Now and again.

Barry He'd just picked up that new suit and couldn't wait to try it on. He walked about our flat buttoning and unbuttoning it, and taking his sunglasses on and off, and standing in strange positions as if he were modelling a deodorant. When he sat down Ra-Ra had just placed her toast on the chair –

Sophie Stephen used to say, these days only a fool isn't a millionaire by forty.

Barry Did he?

Sophie They don't think, every time they open their purse, is there somewhere I can get this cheaper, or do without it. They live at a certain level of freedom in their minds.

Barry Sophie . . . Let's do it – like you said. Move to the country.

Sophie It wouldn't be like this.

Barry What would it be like?

Sophie But even *we* could grow things. We could dig. The children would like the space. Two years we've been talking about it. I'll decide . . .

Barry When?

Sophie Maybe tomorrow. But it could be tonight.

Barry Good. Good. (*Pause.*) I hope no one talks to me.

    A young woman – Lorraine – runs on.

Lorraine (*to Barry*) Hello! How are you? (*She goes to the child.*) Where's your dummy? D'you want your bottle? Good boy. Who's done a poo-poo? Jesus, it's gone right up your back. (*to Sophie and Barry*) I'm Lorraine.

Sophie Sophie and Barry.

Lorraine Right. Julie said.

Sophie Who else is coming? Is . . . erm . . .?

Lorraine I wouldn't know. Not my job.

Sophie I can't wait, I must have a look round . . . Can I?

Lorraine 'Course.

    Sophie goes off, pushing the bicycles.

Barry Sophie . . . (*to Lorraine*) This is all right. Are you staying long?

Lorraine I've got to get you some champagne. I've got to change this kid's clothes. She asked me to show you to your room first. You're in the one with the comfortable bed. You can see the hill, sitting on the toilet. Is it all right if I light the fire later? Sometimes it gets chilly at this time of year. You don't want it now, do you?

Barry My mother used to get up early to light the fires . . . I can do all that.

Lorraine I'm telling you from experience, people are never in the mood late at night. Where's your bags? Sorry. I've got a headache.

Barry What hours does she make you work?

Lorraine Twenty-four hours.

Barry No!

Lorraine In effect, down here. Usually I have the eldest kid in my room all night. All day there's both of them. And the housework . . .

Barry What overtime do you get?

Lorraine What d'you mean?

Barry Anything on top of your basic wage?

Lorraine Nothing.

Barry Terrible.

Lorraine I get to use the other car. It's a convertible. We go to Umbria in the summer. I've pushed that pram up most of the hills of Italy. I want to go to Holland next year. Antigua in the winter. Haven't you been there with them? Here at weekends. In London she's always making me go to concerts, theatre, opera –

Barry Exploitation.

Lorraine picks up his and Sophie's bags.

Lorraine You got kids?

Barry Two. One's six and the other's three and a half. And a third, a girl who lives with us, by my previous. She's twenty.

Lorraine And you didn't bring them or the nanny?

Barry Nanny!

Lorraine Thought I might have someone to talk to.

Barry Talk to me.

Lorraine What are you?

Barry Teacher.

From inside there are voices.

Lorraine Bring the baby, then. We've never had anyone arrive on a bicycle before. There's a shed you can leave it in.

Barry pushes the buggy off; Lorraine takes the bags.

Barry How old are you?

Lorraine Twenty. And you?

Barry Sort of . . . quite late.

Lorraine What's happened to this? (*She looks at the ruck-sack.*)

Barry God, the wine bottle's smashed!

Lorraine I'll have to wash these clothes. There'll be something of Stephen's you can change into. He's got enough clothes down here . . .

Barry No, no . . . please . . .

As they go off Sophie comes out.

Lorraine They dress for dinner . . . She loves to have everything nice . . . I don't blame her. I would. Makes it special. This is going to be a special night . . .

Barry It's not . . . is it? Why?

Julie comes out to join Sophie.

7

Julie Sorry . . . Did you see the view? Try some of this French cheese.

Sophie I'm hungry. Lovely.

Julie D'you think so? Stephen's very irritating at the moment. It's that film, I think. I don't want him to give it to Charles to produce. Stephen's too loyal, that's the problem. I'd like an American. We could live in the States for a year. Mind you, my company is about to make me a producer.

Sophie Really? Won't that be a lot of work?

Julie Where's Barry?

Sophie With Lorraine.

Julie Already? Will he be all right here? I'll talk to him a bit. (*Opens champagne and pours it.*) Is his awful daughter still living with you? Where does she sleep? Stephen told me –

Sophie Joy – that's her name, I'm afraid – has been on methadone since Barry pulled her out of the massage parlour. Which means, of course, that she has no money. She sleeps, when she does sleep, on the sofa in the front room. Our girls have a bedroom between them and we're in that hole off the kitchen. It's stifling. I'm not there most nights.

Julie You're still in the old people's home?

Sophie Wiping old arses, as Stephen would say. It means I can be with the children during the day. You can't imagine the despair and –

Julie Yes?

Sophie The regret and anger that so many of them feel.

Julie I wish I could do something. But I can't, can I? I'll ask . . . Charles if there's any work around. Except that he's ridiculous. The way he says 'hello, darling' and kisses me as if he knows me. He's been hanging around here for three days eating everything and saying it's delicious. He doesn't walk, he trips. People have been taking him seriously since he got that last film of Stephen's made. He goes to festivals in a sky blue suit, taking the credit. Stephen says to him, your film is doing well.

Sophie Julie – Stephen has been helpful. He sent me to see Russell.

Julie You went to university with him.

Sophie I hadn't seen him . . . not once, except on television, until the other day.

Charles comes out.

Julie He's coming to talk to me about a project.

Sophie He's coming is he . . . Alone?

Julie It's just television he knows about. He's not any good with women unless they can whistle the theme tune to *Doctor Who*. (*Pause.*) Does Barry look at you?

Sophie He still wants me to be with him the whole time. He sort of follows me round . . . He'll do anything for me . . .

Julie Really . . . (*Notices Charles.*) Oh God.

Charles (*to Sophie*) Hello, darling. (*He kisses her.*) Stephen's writing. He's almost half-way through. He's going to let me read some of it – if I do what he says. The work he's doing now . . . he's at the height of his powers.

Julie Are you at the height of your powers?

Charles I'm so relaxed these days I'm hardly alive. Are you in therapy?

Julie Everybody talks about themselves enough as it is.

9

Charles That's because it's the one thing most people know anything about.

Stephen comes on. Charles goes to him.

Julie It's the opposite, I would have thought . . .

Charles (*to Stephen*) When can I read it? It will be this weekend, won't it?

Stephen (*to Sophie*) Sophie. Oh . . . you . . . you . . . The kids are well?

Sophie (*to Stephen*) I miss them already.

Stephen (*to Sophie*) You've cut your hair. What has happened?

Sophie What d'you mean?

Julie (*to Charles*) Don't push him too hard.

Charles (*to Julie*) I've never known him have more energy.

Julie (*to Charles*) Everybody wants something from him.

Charles Do you? He always does what he wants. I've learned that from him.

Julie Is that why your life has collapsed?

Charles I've given him my own money to write this film. If I don't sell it this autumn –

Julie You might have to do some work.

Stephen (*to Charles*) I can't get the middle right.

Charles Excellent.

Julie (*going off*) Lorraine!

Charles The last time we talked it was the beginning.

Julie (*towards Lorraine*) What are you doing . . . if anything . . .

Charles (*to Sophie*) How . . . what . . . you . . . Comrade.

Sophie Comrade.

Charles Had a look round?

Sophie I couldn't resist going through the house. (*to Stephen*) The money you must spend on food, wine and champagne. The piles of new books and CDs, cupboards full of clothes, boxes of toys –

Stephen The wood panelling . . .

Sophie There's too much of everything.

Stephen Poverty is the one thing money can't buy.

Pause.

Charles You know the divorce rate? It was in this morning's paper. People are fleeing one another in droves.

Stephen Usually because they're running towards other people.

Charles That's hope for you. You'd think they'd be off straight away . . . But people put up with things, even when they know they won't improve. And when they finally pluck up the courage to leave, it's considered cruel. These days, it's as if people are looking for a rule. If they could decide what the rules are, they'd know where they were.

Stephen Charles, I'm glad you're here. (*He walks with Sophie.*)

Sophie If only Barry wouldn't give everything away.

Stephen Who does he give it to?

Sophie To his parents and eldest daughter. To the parents of poor children in his class. To the Party and to beggars on the street. Still, we're not starving. I despise greed.

Stephen What do you like?

Sophie He's a . . . good man. Children adore him.

Stephen That's no excuse. You have a mind that can move in interesting directions . . . It's wearing, having to think about money constantly. I'm rarely amazed by how much people ask of life, but I am often surprised by how little they ask.

Sophie We weren't so materialistic. We were educated, independent women who didn't need men. Now I can see what use you might have been. (*Pause.*) I blame you for everything. Fifteen years ago I was working as a journalist. You said, they're hollow men with the morals of bailiffs. Better do something real. I went into social work.

Charles I think I'm too relaxed to move. Lorraine, Lorraine – bring me something nice!

Stephen (*to Sophie*) What about . . . You know, I've been thinking of you.

Sophie Do you, sometimes?

Stephen Why not get a lover? Winter's coming on. It would give you something to do during those hours of the day when life has no meaning. And cheer us both up.

Sophie It would be lovely to have someone make you feel beautiful on Wednesdays. It's almost impossible to find anyone to talk to you at all. I'll never be free of the children until it's too late. I'm exhausted already . . . I ache . . . I'm weary . . .

Stephen I would never see Russell voluntarily, but I did phone him and he even took my call. He seems to have become even more important – as Julie, no doubt, will explain.

Sophie He rang me too. I saw him.

Stephen You did?

Barry comes out.

(*to Barry*) Have you got a drink?

Barry Some people have it all right.

Charles Didn't you know? What is happening in education these days?

Stephen (*calls*) Lorraine!

Barry (*to Charles*) Last week I got a punch in the mouth. The kid couldn't speak . . . he was trying to tell me something –

Charles What will happen?

Barry He'll have to go. You see . . . they could learn. They want to learn. The thing is, half the time we're trying to deal with the damage done –

Charles By society?

Barry By the parents. The broken homes.

He goes to sit with Charles. Charles, writing a letter, ignores him.

Charles (*to Barry*) I'm writing a letter.

Barry wanders offstage into the garden.

Stephen (*to Sophie*) So you went?

Sophie I did, but I was afraid . . . I don't meet people like that now.

Stephen Russell was only in my seven and a half hour college production of *The Remembrance of Things Past* because of you – Albertine in a long white dress. Which duchess did I have him play? Was it all of them?

Sophie It would have appalled us to think that that is

how people get on – a word to someone you shared a dressing-room with at university. (*Pause.*) Russell works in a glass and steel building with underlit floors. You feel you're walking on light, or nothing. I had to go through two offices full of women before I got to him. He took me to one of those dark places in Soho. We started drinking whisky macs and beer. He invited me to his flat. It's massive, with nothing in it but televisions. He kept asking me whether I still wore workman's boots. He wanted to strip me. He didn't understand that . . . older women don't enjoy being looked at. My pubic hair's turning grey.

Stephen I am sorry.

Sophie Kindly he turned off the lights and put on a Crosby, Stills and Nash album. 'Let's pretend we're eighteen,' he said. He fucked me really hard. 'I always wanted to do that,' he said. Then we went to the *Magic Flute*, where he had a box. It was . . . my first . . . slip-up. The only time in seven years with Barry.

Stephen What did you think about?

Sophie I saw the children's faces and kept wondering what they were doing. (*Pause.*) There's a lot I want to do. Paint, and grow marrows. What makes you think that it is only passion that people want? (*Pause.*) I know – You must have someone new. Usually you bring them round so they believe you know ordinary people. Why have you kept her from me?

Stephen I mentioned her when I tried on my suit.

Sophie You were more concerned with your buttons. Tell me something – (*Pause.*) Is it the same girl? Anna, isn't it? The one who put milk in your lemon tea and had never heard of Gauguin. Tell me one thing you like about her. (*Pause.*) Are there so many?

Stephen When I put my arm around her in bed she gives

14

this little sigh which says, I'm all right now, this is where I belong. (*Pause.*) Did he offer you a job?

Sophie I love the company of my children.

Stephen They can't give you what an adult can.

Sophie You've always known what you want to do. For me a certain mood would be sufficient. If I could get a sustained measure of contentment . . . let's say, days and days of it without interruption . . . I would sigh like the girl in your bed.

Stephen There's no contentment without love.

Sophie It is simple for men to argue that people should follow their passion. But who plans the children's meals, thinks of their health, clothes, schooling?

Stephen I get up early, make coffee, go to my desk, put on something by Schubert –

Sophie I think you've made her fall in love with you, bastard.

Stephen Day after day of accumulation, interest, creativity. After twenty years I'm just beginning to see what I'm doing. The satisfactions and frustrations are compelling. With each new idea you start again . . . For years I had to force myself to the desk. Now there is love and some urgency, not only in my work –

Sophie Stephen, you're the luckiest person alive.

Stephen Yes. But . . . I think I'm in love.

Pause.

Sophie Why does it take so long to understand anything?

Stephen Sophie, is it because of Russell you asked if you could come down here?

Sophie I needed to get away. I don't know.

Stephen and Sophie look at one another. Sophie moves to the pond and sits.

Lorraine comes on with champagne and clothes for Barry. She puts the champagne on the table and calls to Barry offstage.

Lorraine Barry! You can try these on for later. The arse might be a little tight.

Charles Why can't I try them on?

Lorraine You shut up!

Charles Let's have another drink. Several drinks! Then you try them on!

Lorraine Dressing up – not my job.

Charles (*imitates her*) Not my job! (*Pause. To Barry*) Talking of education, I had a maths teacher who once gave me rather good advice –

Barry Yes?

Charles Go forth and multiply . . .

Lorraine laughs. Stephen moves towards them, listening.

(*to Barry*) Like you, probably, I couldn't take any more. That's what I'm saying in this letter to my eldest son. How do people stay together? Look at me –

Barry Yes –

Charles I'm taking it easy now –

Barry Yes –

Charles But I was waking up in the night shaking, sweating . . . I'm dying already, I thought, and before I've acclimatized. I left home, after fifteen years –

16

Barry You did?

Charles Years too late . . . My marriage was basically a one-night stand that went on too long. The children don't speak to me. The boy attempted suicide. They put him in a psychiatric hospital. My wife hates me and won't let me in my own house. The woman I love won't leave her husband. My money's gone . . .

Lorraine (*offering a drink*) Get this down you. There's enough here to kill us all.

Charles There's such spirit in your eyes.

Barry (*to Lorraine*) You don't have to put up with that.

Charles Rebel . . . rebel against everything that's dead inside you.

Barry And outside you.

Charles I lived with the dead. I made everything dead –

Lorraine Older people say such strange things . . . I realize it when I go down to the village and see normal people –

Barry Can't we go down there and really laugh?

Lorraine (*to Charles, as he drinks*) If that doesn't work, I'll sing to you!

  Julie comes on.

Julie (*to Stephen*) There you are. I need to talk to you.

Barry (*to Sophie*) I rang home just now. Thought I'd got the wrong number. All I heard was screaming.

Sophie Let's open our wine.

Barry It smashed.

Julie Stephen –

Barry (*slapping his neck*) There's a lot of flies out here . . .

Stephen Is it you in particular they are attracted to?

Julie laughs. Russell comes on, one arm full of newspapers, magazines, scripts and paperwork, the other holding bread, cheese, cakes . . .

Russell Hey, hey . . . hey . . .

Julie You did come!

Russell And just round the corner from Jack. And Roger with his own cutting-room just down the road –

Julie Wonderful. Lorraine –

Lorraine rushes to him and takes the things.

Russell So this is the little place you're buying? It's so big I couldn't find my way in.

Stephen What?

Russell Better sharpen your pencil!

Charles Yes.

Russell greets everyone.

Stephen Lorraine – alcohol.

Barry I'll get it. She's got a headache.

Stephen No, she hasn't. (*to Lorraine*) You can put those down. Off you go, Miss Not-My-Job . . .

Lorraine goes off.

Barry (*to Stephen*) How can you talk to her like that?

Russell (*giving Sophie a bag*) You are here. I wondered. Are you –

Sophie It's good to see you.

18

Russell Open it.

Sophie This is Barry, who I live with.

Stephen (*to Russell*) You haven't met before?

Russell (*to Barry*) Russell.

Charles (*to Stephen*) Aren't you going to do any more work today?

Julie He was up at six. He'll make himself mad.

Sophie I want to have a luxurious bath and a lie down.

Barry With me? I'll run it for you. Come on –

Julie There you go.

Sophie I want someone to read poetry to me while I lie there drinking champagne and eating crackers . . . And never move again . . .

Barry Where do they keep the poetry . . .

Stephen Everywhere. 'It is too late to depart/For destinations not of the heart . . .'

> *Barry goes off.*
>   *Russell goes to Sophie as she is about to follow Barry. Julie watches.*
>   *Sophie opens the bag. It is an antique scarf.*

Russell Soph. Thank you for coming to see me. I . . . Did you like it?

Sophie (*looking at the scarf*) It's beautiful . . . Thank you, thanks. (*She kisses him.*)

Russell Work with me.

Sophie You want me to . . .

Russell . . . I've decided to go ahead with the film about American education. Go to Boston and talk to them.

Sophie Give me a chance . . . Can I let you know?

Russell Say now . . . just for fun.

Sophie I want to. But I can't . . . The children –

Russell Tomorrow morning. Right?

Sophie All right. Yes. All right.

She goes off.
  Charles and Russell together.

Charles (*to Russell*) Congratulations.

Russell Thanks. I started that company in one room. Not long ago people were still sitting on the floor.

Stephen And you sold it to Retview.

Russell I can't even think about what they paid for it.

Charles Will they let you do what you want?

Russell Features, serials, documentaries . . . Then movies. Nothing too arty or difficult. They'll let me alone as long as I give them product that people will watch.

Julie goes to Stephen.

Julie (*to Stephen*) To be in that position at his age, with that money behind him. He'll be one of the top people in Europe. Stephen . . .

Stephen (*to Julie*) What do you want?

Julie I need to talk to you now.

Lorraine brings on a bottle.

Charles I'm opening this. Unless you want to go for a . . . walk –

Russell Walk?

Charles Sorry.

Russell They're all the same, these tree places.

Charles London without pavements.

Russell A couple of hours and you're wishing –

Charles Minutes . . .

Russell Wellington boots . . .

Charles Anyhow, I'm writing to my son. (*Pause.*) You must be looking for brilliant new projects?

Russell Oh yes.

Charles I'll put my thinking cap on then.

Russell looks through the newspapers. Charles writes a letter.

Julie (*to Stephen*) I invited a lot of people this weekend – proper people, apart from Russell – but they can't come.

Stephen Because they don't like you?

Julie You've argued with everyone else . . . or insulted them! That's why we had to invite Sophie and Barry. But it's also because people have their own houses . . . which they bought. I've been saying we have to make a decision about this place quite soon, Monday, otherwise they'll put it on the market. What do you say?

Stephen Why buy it?

Julie Useless – we've discussed this! I've come to love this house and the time we spend here together with the children . . . (*Pause.*) Might we go to America?

Stephen You have no idea how much everything costs, probably because, despite your education –

Julie I won a scholarship, thank you, and fought for a place – unlike Charles, who –

Stephen . . . And your considerable pretensions, you've always earned so little yourself. You just spend and spend . . . I'm going to have to take jobs I don't want –

Julie Oh dear. Like everyone else. But you've made money. I don't know how much. What you don't have is any sense of family –

Stephen I hate fucking families!

Julie I am beginning to despise you . . . I supported you while you got off that dirty stuff . . . The times you've been crawling on your knees banging your head on the floor.

Stephen I'll let you know . . . about the house.

Julie Oh . . . if only people knew you!

Stephen You – your snobbery – And it's like going to bed with a semi-inflated dinghy –

Julie Contempt – (*Pause.*) I rang little Joe at his grandma's just now.

Stephen Is he all right? I feel guilty about sending him away this weekend.

Julie This morning, before he went, he pulled up my jumper and plunged his hands into my breasts. What are these, he said. I said, what d'you think, little man. Toys, he announced.

Stephen (*laughing*) Last night he was drumming on the table. I said, what are you doing. Singing with my fingers, he replied.

Julie Ah . . . You love the children.

Stephen Your anger is unbearable.

Julie You make me like this. You don't let me in.

Stephen You wouldn't like what you saw.

Julie takes Russell off.

Julie (*to Russell*) I'm sorry, but no one else has arrived. Peter's coming, I promise, and he's got a pretty girl staying with him. Talk to me. Guess who I saw the other night.

Russell Oh no . . . Where were you?

Julie After the screening we all went out to supper – They were saying how jealous of you they were . . .

Russell So they should be –

Julie and Russell exit.

Stephen (*to Charles*) I've decided . . .

Charles Good, good. The indecision about this house has been getting on my nerves. You can settle down and work here and –

Stephen Tonight will be the last . . . Bring on the lawyers, I'm leaving tomorrow.

Charles Where?

Stephen I'm leaving my wife and children. I suppose I should . . . I should inform them – or at least her. Yes, I must do that. I will do that. Yes. What we need . . . I'm convinced of it . . . is a little honesty. A little straightfor-wardness. The thing is, I can't stop myself despising her . . . We can't satisfy one another . . . not for one moment. It would be sensible to give up –

Charles If one were sensible. But you have a good arrangement. Wife, healthy children, money, mistresses –

Stephen An infidelity a day keeps the doctor away. Some betrayals are absolutely necessary . . . But I liked her, Anna. I can't remember why I liked Julie. We used to laugh. But I'm no longer curious about her. There has to be that at least, don't you think? Love is a kind of curiosity. I might come and stay with you for a while. I used to think that leaving home was something you did only once – But you've got irritating habits and no books.

Charles You could write one. When did you last see the girl?

Stephen It's been a month. She's had enough. She's seeing other men now. I couldn't ask her not to.

Charles Yes, you could. Ask, ask –

Stephen She wants me out of her mind. Anyhow, I am going to smash everything up, destroy Julie, the family . . . the children. (*Pause.*) If this really is the end . . . I want to . . . not exactly savour it . . . but notice it, and Julie. I want to get at, if I can, what it was I wanted her for.

Charles It's so violent, leaving – Our fathers didn't leave. I'd notice men, after I left . . . with their children, just on the street, going to the pictures . . . holding hands . . . Stephen . . . it broke me.

Lorraine comes on and hands Stephen a bib, a bowl and a spoon.

Lorraine It's time for Sean to eat. You said you wanted to feed him.

Stephen Yes, he sort of sings when he eats. He's so succulent. I could put him in a sandwich with mustard and pickle and bite into his arse –

Lorraine He threw his breakfast down.

Stephen Was it that broccoli you do?

Lorraine Joe bites and kicks me. Some of the other nannies are very firm –

Stephen They're God's breath to me, those children. They

24

enchant me. I like being a father. It's being a husband that disagrees with me.

Lorraine You don't spend every moment of the day with them – They never stop wanting . . .

Stephen Did you get down to the village for that stuff?

Lorraine Oh yes. (*She hands Stephen a small envelope.*)

Stephen Good girl. (*to Charles*) I thought I noticed Lorraine moving rather too rapidly just now.

Charles Doing something that wasn't her job?

Stephen Joe said to me yesterday, why is mummy cross all the time? (*Pause.*) What must there be? Love. What is it we want and need? Love. What is the only sustenance and the deepest pleasure of all? Love. Why? I don't know. How banal . . . I'm sick of myself . . . I want to be some-one else . . . I'm going to speak to Julie . . . so she knows . . . It's the best thing I've ever done, and the worst . . . The thing is – she's not really my type . . . Where's my lit-tle boy? (*He goes.*)

Lorraine I'll tell you a story.

Charles That would be lovely . . .

Lorraine But not now . . . later, tonight . . . You said I had nice eyes. What did you mean by that?

Charles There's more to you than you let yourself know . . .

Lorraine They're sweet words. Where d'you get them from?

Charles They'd been lying around in my mind . . . You cheer me up . . . My son said to me, what did you do in the sixties? It was the seventies really. The revolution came late to some of us. My wife was a feminist . . . you won't remember all that, women hating one on principle. I even hated myself on principle. She thought affection was capitalist . . . even a smile was a class betrayal . . . I went along with it . . . I want to remember everything. I lived in a house with people who made bombs and blew things up . . . I remember planning to kidnap an industrialist and cut off his ears . . .

Lorraine You didn't!

Charles I was saved by cowardice . . . Odd how most of the conflicts our families have been involved in have been between people who have lived in close proximity to one another . . . People who found it easier to kill one another than talk . . . It's proximity that's impossible . . .

Lorraine What's proximity? (*Pause. He pinches her.*) Ouch . . .

Charles You've got to work. But wait for me by the river later . . .

Lorraine Really?

Charles Yes . . . And I'll polish up some more words for you . . .

They go off.

SCENE TWO

In the garden, food is gradually being brought out on to tables – by Lorraine and Julie – where there will be a buffet.

Russell works rapidly through a pile of newspapers, ripping out the bits he wants to keep, stuffing the cuttings in his pockets, throwing the rest down . . . while, perhaps, Lorraine clears up the rest . . .

Julie (*to Russell*) They repeated the Fellini interview. What time did you stop watching? You can get a tape and fast forward through it. I saw Jeremy after, in the Blue Café. I had to give Stephen's name to get in. It's getting like New York. This fashion thing's gone too far. Pete and Roger were at the next table, avoiding people, with Joanne. She's doing it with the poet, can you believe it?

Russell The one with the hair?

Julie Lorraine! (*Pause.*) No, he wears green shorts. Everyone hated that last book, apart from people who like poetry. I had to see Andrew. He's buying that story . . . I want to work on it. They're making that film with all the furniture, with Yves' money. I had the black squid. Have you had the cappuccino brûlée in The Ivy? Can't we send for one now? As Stephen said, it's like going down on the whole of the Manchester United first team at once –

Russell Oh yuck, oh God . . . He's been so promiscuous for so long . . .

Julie How do you know . . .

Russell What?

Julie That he's been like that?

Russell Been like what?

Julie Promiscuous. Who told you? Did he tell you himself?

Russell I never see him really.

Julie Well, then . . . how . . .

Russell My diary's stuffed with meetings but . . . how about if we went shopping for a couple of hours next week? I've got a driver now, and a Mercedes. He can follow us around and we can stick the bags in the back. I usually prefer the bags to the clothes.

Julie (*to Lorraine*) Don't put that there! Put it down!

Lorraine What? What am I doing?

Julie For God's sake!

Russell Peter's not going to come now. He must have gone to Janet's. We'll get by. I've invited a friend over for supper.

Julie (*to Lorraine*) Stupid! (*to Russell*) What does she do?

Russell Just started work in the office. She really likes me. I think this one might go. I'd love to know what you think. Have a good look at her. You will tell me, won't you? You know I respect your judgement.

Julie I shouldn't have given the room with the comfortable bed to Barry and Sophie.

Russell I'll take her across to Janet's tomorrow.

Julie Why?

Russell She's got a swimming pool.

Julie We've got a river.

Russell I don't like rivers.

Julie What do you like?

Barry comes on as Lorraine rushes off.

Russell Is she relaxing?

Barry I ran the bath. I found a poem. But she's parked herself in front of that big mirror. I can't get her away from it.

Julie Really? She's looking at herself . . .

Barry In a sort of dream . . .

Russell She won't have much time for that when she starts for me. People don't have jobs now – they join other families and they're in the office till eight. Then there's drinks and supper. You'd have thought there'd be less work around. Don't worry – she'll be better paid than you.

Barry Will she?

Russell You know what my teacher used to say? That boy will never do anything – all he does is watch television. Have you tried this bread?

Julie Here's some oil. And olives. Lorraine! Barry, will you open this for me?

Russell (*to Barry*) Only Stephen would have an au pair with a pair like that. This is the life, eh? My father's a taxi driver. On the way to Paris the train goes through the station where he works, and sometimes I see him parked outside – And I wave!

> *Lorraine goes outside. Barry watches her and then follows her.*

Julie (*to Russell*) If he's going to be miserable and boring I'll slap him. He didn't have to come. It was Stephen's idea.

Russell . . . So Sophie lives with him . . . Do they get along?

Julie Yes. Why? (*Pause.*) Is she really going to work for you? But why?

Russell I thought it a good idea to have someone in the office who's actually lived in the world . . . I'm going to have to fire some of the idiots now.

Julie You never went out with Sophie . . . or did you?

Russell I saw her on my first day at university. I watched her for three years . . . and how she changed. Her father was a poor farmer. She met Stephen in the first week. He

29

was very aloof . . . you know. They became this ravishing, brilliant couple . . . She dyed her hair vermilion and wore shades and workman's boots to classes on Wittgenstein . . . Then they'd be off to dinner with musicians and directors and transvestites . . . giving the impression they were doing us a favour being in the building at all . . . while we just went to the library . . .

Sophie And you thought –

Russell Yes . . . I thought . . . why can't I have a woman like that –

Julie And why couldn't you?

Russell They'd always want to be somewhere else. (*Pause.*) Don't you remember her from later?

Julie Only that he kept running off to her.

Russell You put a stop to it?

Julie I had to.

She goes into the house. Russell follows her. Barry has joined Lorraine in the garden.

Lorraine I burnt myself again. I'm shaking . . .

Barry (*taking her hand*) I am. These people remind me of what it is we're up against. (*Pause.*) Ask them for a pay rise. Ask for fifty per cent. Hit them hard. After that you can compromise.

Lorraine You think she'll agree?

Barry Oh yes . . . If she values you . . .

Lorraine I'm nervous.

Barry That's what they want. But you make everything work here . . .

Lorraine Will you help me?

Barry I'll be right beside you. People don't know their own strength until they've scared people with it. (*He kisses her burnt hand.*)

Julie (*off*) Lorraine!

Barry (*to Lorraine*) Be firm! I'm here.

Lorraine Fifty per cent! Is that double?

She exits into the house, leaving cushions on a chair as she goes. Barry wanders off. Charles and Stephen come on.

Charles Do they sleep with you, the kids?

Stephen Most nights they end up between us . . . Sometimes I can pick out my wife in her white nightie in the distance, across the bridge of bodies . . .

Charles It's them you'll miss sleeping with.

Sophie – having changed for the evening – comes in and looks at the dinner table.

Stephen She moves me so, Sophie . . . more than ever.

Charles . . . I don't understand it . . . I've never known a man more adored . . . If it were me I'd sink up to my neck in kisses, hair, breasts . . .

Stephen You should never have let me leave the Norwegian au pair.

Charles I remember, the push into Europe.

Stephen Twice a week at your place . . . she removed my shoes, rubbed my head . . . told me my work was under-estimated –

Charles You wouldn't listen to me –

Stephen There are some fucks for which a man would watch his wife and children drown in a freezing sea.

31

Twice. But I'm finished with all that. I was looking for something I couldn't possibly find. (*Pause.*) I've changed my mind.

Charles Sorry?

Stephen Any fool can fall in love. It's living with someone, for a long time . . . That's the impossible thing or duty, that everyone wants, that everyone has to do. You can't just run away. And it's easier, you know, to live with someone you don't love.

Charles No, no . . .

Stephen You wouldn't know. I'm going to tell Anna, if I ever see her again, that it's off . . . over. What I want now are the mature, profounder consolations . . .

Charles Please remind me –

Stephen Contentment, I was thinking of. (*Pause.*) It might seem strange to you but I felt an erection coming on, earlier. I never get erections in the country.

Charles Does anyone?

Stephen If only my wife were attractive . . .

Charles Can't you finish the film first?

Stephen If you help me find a new girlfriend I might show you some of it.

Charles But since you saw Anna and had the jolt . . . well, you haven't been interested . . .

Stephen I didn't let them touch me . . . that was the point . . .

Charles All I want is for you to be emotionally comfortable.

Stephen Yes, yes. Thank you.

Charles While you finish the film.

They go off.
Russell enters, talking on his mobile phone.

Russell (*to Sophie*) I won't be long. (*on the phone*) You're not that far away . . . No . . .

Barry enters from the garden, sees Sophie, and goes to her.

Barry (*to Sophie*) There you are –

Sophie What's that?

Barry The cracker and the poem you asked for . . . that I've been trying to give you . . .

Lorraine enters from the house with cutlery.

Lorraine (*to Barry*) You'd better get changed into those clothes. Julie will get very annoyed if you come to dinner looking like that.

Russell (*on the phone*) Tell the driver to just keep going! I can't wait to see you . . . Yes . . . Nice people, good food, some of my employees, and me. I know you're not used to this kind of thing . . . but we don't have to stay long . . . And tomorrow we'll go swimming and then to the Albert Hall to see . . .

Barry Sophie . . .

Sophie What?

Russell Good. She's coming. She wants me.

Sophie Does she? And you?

Russell (*going back into the house*) I don't mind. Maybe. Let me know what you think. You know I respect your judgement.

Barry (*to Lorraine*) Did you speak to her?

Lorraine No.

Barry You're tough. You can do it.

Lorraine Julie – Julie –

Barry leads Sophie into the garden.

Barry (*to Sophie*) I've been thinking . . . You look lovely . . . your hair's shining . . . What's that?

Sophie . . . Out here I can breathe . . .

Barry . . . Perfume, too. Is it Julie's? (*Pause.*) I want you to know . . . I've been trying to say . . . I love you . . . I always have. And I admire and respect your intelligence and feeling for others. And I love our life together . . . despite, you know . . . We've got nothing like this. There are always difficulties . . . as Stephen says, the moment two people say hello it's going to be hell . . . I'll ask my daughter to leave, if it's getting you down. But sometimes you just have to take care of people . . . I wondered if there was something . . . will you tell me something . . . To say this is hard, hard for me –

Sophie I went to see Russell. Last week. I used to know him.

Barry I know. But you didn't tell me. He gave you a present. Why? Did you agree to anything?

Sophie He asked me to work for him. My own office, a good salary.

Barry You'd have to go in every day?

Sophie I'd go to Boston to help with a documentary.

Barry In America?

Sophie He's got to make some serious programmes.

Barry But why . . . why would he do this for you?

(*Pause.*) Oh . . . oh, I see.

Sophie No . . . no . . . no . . . I would never –

Barry It's the old boys and girls network . . . class . . .

Sophie Barry, we could buy a house in which we can get dressed without fear of pushing our hands through the window. If you're tired of the school you can stay at home and look after the girls. It is your turn. You can read your book on speed reading . . .

Barry Money isn't everything, Sophie.

Sophie The media has more influence than posters, leaflets, meetings . . . That might be a reason for working within it –

Barry It's a narcotic. A constant onslaught of refuse rotting the soul . . .

Sophie We watch it every night.

Barry You forget the people outside . . . who don't want vets and soap operas –

Sophie What would you like me to do?

Barry What you want – You know I don't like to be alone. After all this time I can't get enough of you . . .

Stephen comes on with his youngest child in his arms, wrapped in a blanket. He walks the child up and down.

Stephen All right, little man . . . my son, little boy, I know how you feel, sleep . . . it's okay . . . Daddy's here, for the moment . . .

Sophie (*to Barry*) Well . . . think it over . . . you too, both of us, until tomorrow. (*Pause.*) You like Lorraine.

Barry These liberals can be very liberal when it comes to certain things but they treat her like a servant.

35

Sophie Try it with her. (*Pause.*) Don't you get tired of saying no to everything? Yes is such a good word. Yes . . . yes . . . (*Pause.*) When Julie started on Stephen she'd send him flowers every day. She'd have dinner parties in order to introduce him to people who'd help him. She praised his work, whereas I just took it for granted. At first he'd say, she'll go to bed with anyone, provided they've recently received a warm review in a decent newspaper. It was when he called her a rabid lapdog that I should have realized she was about to move right into his flat. Before, I'd listen to music in his room while he finished writing. Most nights we'd go to the theatre and to supper with writers and actors. He took me to San Francisco and we drove to Big Sur. I didn't know what a pleasant life it was . . . In the late seventies we became very hardline. There was the authority of the Party –

Barry Overturn all that's established, bring it down . . . Give people a chance to shine, to flourish – that's all it is . . .

Sophie . . . Marriage, family, class . . . they made us slaves of the past . . . So I had affairs with men and some women, we lived in that housing co-op where we had to do all the washing up. We marched and demonstrated . . . and now I live like everyone else . . . (*Pause.*) You can't have freedom once and for all. It has to be renewed every day . . . If you want her, try your luck. You're afraid I'll do the same? There's no one here for me. (*Pause.*) Go and change . . .

Barry Sophie –

Sophie It's only for fun. You're not joining the army.

Barry All right . . . Sleep with me . . . later. Will you? It's been a while . . .

Sophie We can do what we want . . .

Barry Yes is such a good word . . .

He kisses her. He goes.
Pause.

Stephen (*to Sophie*) Russell will be delighted.

Sophie About what?

Stephen To have you in his office.

Sophie No. I'll learn a language instead. Buy me some more boots.

Russell comes on.

Russell I heard a taxi. Is she here?

Stephen Yes.

Stephen points at Sophie. Pause.

Russell Stand next to one another. (*Pause.*) You two . . . both of you . . . Yes. Why couldn't you stay together?

Stephen walks behind with the child.

Sophie I wish I could stay here.

Russell And do what?

Sophie Think . . . read . . . walk . . . be with myself.

Russell Myself, I can't keep still. I have to keep moving . . .

Sophie Yes, there has to be movement . . . (*Pause.*) What you did to me . . . Would you . . . will you . . . be doing it again?

Russell I don't know. Why not? We liked it . . . didn't we? Do you want to? (*Pause.*) If there's time . . .

Pause.

Sophie (*to Stephen*) Let me take him a minute . . . I want to smell a baby again . . .

Stephen passes her the child.

Hello in there . . .

Stephen (*to Russell*) I hear you're going steady at last.

Sophie (*to Russell*) Here. (*She goes to hand him the baby.*)

Russell I wouldn't go that far. And I'm not touching it . . .

Stephen To me, you'll always be a duchess with a dirty nose . . .

Russell I've got so much work to do . . . I haven't got time for normal conversation . . . (*He hurries off.*)

Sophie (*to Stephen*) Come and sit with me. I want to hear more about your work.

Stephen Why . . .

Sophie It reminds me of the good things . . .

Stephen But I'm afraid, Soph. I've lost confidence . . . I write a line and loathe myself for it. She and I sap each other . . . and hate one another's capability . . . Why have we chosen one another for this task?

Sophie I wonder . . .

Stephen The river's high and fast tonight . . . like us. Let's go and look at it.

They walk off.
Julie and Lorraine continue bringing food out on to tables in the garden.

Lorraine . . . Julie . . . Julie . . . I've noticed recently, just talking out loud, that some of the other nannies and au pairs earn more than I do –

Julie They do?

Lorraine Why . . . why . . . is that, d'you think . . . when

I'm no different, in fact, less mad, less likely to drop a child on its head, than some –

Julie I've talked out loud too and ascertained . . . they don't have so many headaches. Those migraines are costing you.

Lorraine Couldn't they be caused by financial worry –

Anna comes on.

Julie (*to Lorraine*) Have you got apple juice? Did you do all their shopping? What have you forgotten?

Anna Hello.

Lorraine Everyone forgets things, Julie –

Julie You've noticed though that I tend not to forget your wages?

Lorraine But Julie . . . how did you get all this without asking for more?

Julie By finding a man to pay for it.

Lorraine I've never met anyone more hard-working than you . . . how you keep everything together, it's a miracle . . .

Anna Is Russell here, please?

Julie Oh. Yes. I think he's upstairs.

Anna Right.

Julie Sorry, I'm Stephen's wife, Julie. This way . . . I think he's reading scripts and watching tapes . . . He's got a lot to do, as you probably know . . . You're in the room next to the children. Only the youngest is here tonight. Would you like to have a peep at him?

Anna I couldn't disturb him –

Julie He's more likely to disturb you . . . He's got a bit of a cold . . . Last night he was up three hours . . .

Julie and Anna go.

SCENE THREE

Music continues . . .
It becomes evening. The food has been brought out.
Lorraine rings the bell. Stephen sitting there with Julie.

Julie We're nearly ready . . . They're not here. I want everyone to eat at once . . .

Stephen They will . . . after a while.

Julie It doesn't matter to you. You just don't care. (*to Lorraine*) Ring it again.

Stephen (*to Julie*) Let me look at your hands.

Julie Do you like my nail varnish? Why stare at me? (*Pause.*) You're old now.

Stephen Already?

Lorraine rings the bell.

Julie You were beautiful once . . . people said . . .

Stephen Aren't my eyes still soft? Isn't there something alive in me? I know there is, underneath.

Julie I haven't noticed . . . I'm sure someone has. Have you made up your mind?

Stephen Sorry?

Sophie and Barry come in.

Stephen (*to Julie*) I like your food.

Julie You never say so. You weren't going to.

Stephen I love your cooking . . . and all this . . . you know . . . the effort and preparation and care that goes into everything you do . . . your love for the children and your kindness . . .

Julie I could produce your film. Let me, Stephen. It'll be you and me again.

Stephen At least, perhaps, we should go for a walk . . .

Julie Why?

Stephen You're right. It's never just you and me. I want to cut through the . . . stupidities and see if we can be honest with one another . . . You know what the most terrifying thing is . . . trying to talk to someone else . . . there are certain conversations and pleasures and intimacies one would rather die than have . . .

Julie Yes. That's right, yes.

Stephen Once, I loved listening to you . . .

Anna, Russell and Charles come in.

Charles (*to Lorraine*) Can't you ring my bell?

Lorraine Do it yourself.

Julie There's people here. Russell's girlfriend. He wants to know what we think. Why don't you kiss me at least? (*Pause.*) I'll close my eyes . . . little Stevie Wonder, my husband . . .

Stephen I've got something in my eye. (*to Charles*) Tomorrow.

Charles Can I tell you something?

Stephen There's nothing I want to know.

Barry, wearing Stephen's clothes, presents himself to Sophie.

41

Barry Is this all right?

Sophie (*to Stephen*) What do you think? Stephen.

Stephen I bought that velvet jacket on Columbus Avenue. I wore it to Sardis when I picked up my New York critics award. It's still got the stain where . . . (*to Anna*) Hello . . . Welcome . . .

Anna Thank you.

Stephen You must see the garden. There are herbs, and horses, and . . . would you like to have a guided tour?

Anna I don't know.

Stephen There's a lot to see here. Let me take you . . .

Russell Anna . . . what am I going to eat? Can you help me choose . . .

Stephen (*to Russell*) You should try Lorraine's broccoli. There.

Sophie (*to Julie, indicating Anna*) Is that her?

Julie The friend?

Sophie Yes.

Julie Of course.

Sophie Yes.

Julie I see.

Sophie Well.

Julie Yes.

Sophie Okay.

   Pause.

Russell (*to Julie*) Thank you, Julie, for inviting us all here . . .

Sophie Yes! Hurrah!

Barry Up you all! . . .

Lorraine And you –

Julie Eat, eat . . . get stinking drunk and fall on top of one another! . . . Lorraine –

Sophie Stephen –

Russell Anna –

Stephen Charles –

Charles Yes, my darling . . .

Music . . . Everyone eats and talks . . . Their voices continue on the track as we change scene . . .

SCENE FOUR

Later, and deeper in the garden Julie drinks her coffee. Stephen joins her and touches her.

Stephen Russell looks like an undertaker –

Julie He doesn't –

Stephen It's the pompous dignity, combined with the utter emptiness of effortless success . . .

Julie He propositioned me.

Stephen He did?

Julie He wanted to know if you were jealous . . . I said, very, but explained that it didn't matter . . .

Stephen Russell propositions everyone. An undertaker needs bodies . . . Anyway, he said, when I'm dressed I'm thinking and when I'm undressed I'm dreaming . . .

43

Julie Charles?

Stephen Our son. (*in child's voice*) You know, in this world, I was finking . . . when I'm dressed I'm . . .

They laugh.

Julie Don't you love watching them change? (*Pause.*) Charles is irritating. I've never understood why your closest friends are such cripples . . .

Stephen His own mind appals him . . . the world is inexplicable to him. Every day he's puzzled by everything. (*He touches Julie.*)

Julie Why do you enjoy such indulgence?

Stephen It shows a certain curiosity about the difficulty of living –

Julie I'll know you've changed when you're not bothered with Charles any more. (*Pause.*) I spoke to the architect this afternoon . . . Why d'you keep doing that?

Stephen I'd just as soon never touch you again. Or see you again, for that matter.

Julie Good, because we're going to build a study for you with a wooden floor and rugs, and a separate library in the barn, with a music system. I don't like you drinking in that summer-house in the middle of the night. You'd still be living out of cardboard boxes . . . You don't have much to say to me.

Stephen There was something . . .

Anna and Russell join them.

How things harden between people . . . and can't be softened – And how cruel you find yourself becoming . . . without wanting to be . . .

Julie (*to Anna and Russell*) We're going to buy it . . . you two can come here whenever you like . . .

Russell I think I might get my own. (*to Anna*) What do you think? Would you like a place like this?

Anna I'd love it . . . if it were somewhere else.

Russell Yes.

Charles comes on.

Julie (*to Anna*) How is your room?

Anna . . . Yes . . . thank you . . . fine –

Julie Lorraine will get you some towels. I'll have her light the fire in case it gets cold later. It shouldn't do. I think it will be a lovely night. Stephen and I slept in there when we first took the house . . . Stephen would get up and write at the desk in the morning . . . and I'd lie in bed listening to his ideas . . . keeping him going . . .

Stephen (*to Anna*) I like your ear-rings.

Anna Thank you.

Julie (*to Charles*) You didn't eat much, for you. Aren't you relaxed?

Stephen (*to Anna*) Who gave them to you?

Charles (*to Julie*) I'm less relaxed than I have been, to tell you the truth . . . In fact –

Anna A friend.

Russell kisses Anna. She whispers in his ear. Anna goes off.

Stephen Was it a good friend, an acquaintance, or someone just passing through?

Russell Tell them how much you liked *The Magic Flute*. You were humming it earlier.

45

Anna goes off.

She wants to get some air.

Stephen Right.

Russell Don't worry, she's from the suburbs but she likes the country. It's the people she's not used to . . .

Stephen Yes, we make her feel that she doesn't know who she is.

Julie She's pretty.

Stephen Do you think so? (*to Russell*) Where did you meet her?

Russell Girls just walk into the office all day. (*Pause.*) How long is it you've been married? I was thinking the other day that it's time I did it.

Julie This one? I don't believe it.

Russell It's early days, but . . . I don't want any excitement.

Charles No!

Julie Five and a half years. It was in the garden of the Cipriani in Venice . . . They do this wonderful thing . . . They bound our hands together with white silk thread . . . the candles were joined . . . making one flame . . .

Stephen Funny how marriage has become more of an exhibition than an institution –

Julie Have you decided?

Stephen Oh yes . . .

Julie (*to Russell*) He said yes. We're buying it . . .

Russell (*raises his glass*) Here's to that, then.

Stephen (*imitating him*) Here's to that, then . . .

Stephen leaves, following Anna.

Russell Everybody's started being nice to me now. It makes me uncomfortable. Got any ideas for programmes?

Julie What will you give me for them?

Russell Stop it.

Charles There's this film I want to do with Stephen. I was looking for a bit of development money –

Russell You know I'd be interested . . . What's the story this time?

Charles Er . . .

Russell Come on. Pitch it. We'll do the deal and that'll be that.

Charles Yes. I see.

Russell So?

Charles I'll tell you later . . . tonight or at breakfast.

Russell I won't hang around.

Charles No. But I must . . . I need to consult with the writer.

Russell Why would anyone want to consult the writer?

Julie Russell –

Charles fetches coffee.

Charles Anyone else?

Julie (*to Russell*) I want to ask you something.

Russell Wait one minute. She's probably gone up to the room. Sweetheart!

He goes off at the side to look for her. Julie takes something into the house.

47

Sophie and Barry walking through.

Sophie It's still warm . . . but in the morning there'll be a mist. Autumn's my favourite season . . . out here you can smell and feel the changes . . .

Barry Let's find a place to sleep out tonight . . . We can take a blanket and lie under the stars and talk and touch and . . .

Sophie Where are the others?

Barry . . . Even if we don't sleep we could lie down in the grass for a bit and try to remember who we are . . .

Sophie I want to talk . . .

Barry To Russell?

Sophie Anyone – I think I've forgotten what other people are like. How mad and strange and disturbing they are. We've become so isolated . . .

Barry Let's find the river . . . just for a minute –

Sophie Okay. But don't be long . . .

Barry Sophie –

Sophie goes in another direction. He walks alone towards the river. As Julie comes out, Russell rejoins her.

Julie Is she still on the loose?

Russell She's really very keen on me. I'm going to take her to Cannes.

Julie (*to Russell*) Russell, do you hear . . . round and about in London, much about Stephen?

Russell A journalist rang only the other day asking –

Julie You know then, where he goes and what he does . . . and the sort of people he is with.

Russell People say . . . he works most of the time . . . He's getting quite a reputation . . . as a writer – That's what they talk about, Julie.

Julie Tell me if you know any more. I need to know . . .

Sophie joins them.

Russell If you find a good man, hold on to him . . . Isn't that what they say? (*Calls.*) Anna! (*Pause.*) We're the lucky ones, Charles . . . Unattached. We can come and go as we want. Don't you ever think about that, Julie?

Julie It's been so long . . . I don't remember what it's like. My father ran out of the front door one night when I was young . . . Two minutes later he came back for the television, which he couldn't quite carry. He left it in the front garden . . . He came and went as he wanted but it didn't cheer him up . . . I wouldn't want to be alone, and I don't want to be with a lot of men. The family is a point you can live from. I like ordinary, everyday life . . . laying the table, being in this house, choosing furniture . . . shopping for food . . .

Charles (*to Sophie*) Do you like that?

Russell She's thinking . . .

Sophie I don't know . . . If there isn't enough money . . . We're up to our necks in debt and we can't stop working. I wish I knew how to find some pleasure . . . You obviously can.

Julie Yes . . . a little . . . I've always wanted a family . . . to disappear into.

Sophie That's the mistake, though – thinking you can find everything there . . . Families, if you don't mind me saying so, are mental hospitals.

Julie What else is there? Lorraine's removed the cheesecake. Shall we go and find it? It could be anywhere. I find a lot of food under her bed.

Charles (*to Russell as they all go off*) And you think you'll definitely be interested in Stephen's idea . . .

Stephen approaches Anna.

Anna It's a lovely place . . .

Stephen I suppose it is . . . Do you remember what you said when I gave you those ear-rings? Did you get them yourself? Sorry?, I said. Did you actually walk into the shop?, you said. You thought I'd sent Charles for them –

Anna Do you remember what you said? It must have been the third time we met. I'm at your disposal.

Stephen Did I?

Anna Thank you for your letters. This is where you write them. You've got all your things here. I'd like to see every-thing, your notebooks and pens and books, and hear the music you play. And that's Sophie . . .

Stephen I've been meaning to take you to see her.

Anna Is that what happens to people? I wouldn't want to be one of those old confused women flapping about at forty, still wondering who they are –

Stephen She was beautiful.

Anna Don't make me jealous and horrible.

Stephen Marry me then.

Anna Stephen – I will. I can't.

Stephen Marry me and I'll never leave you again, not for one minute . . . I'll be on top of you until you're sick of me . . .

Anna Sometimes I think you are making a fool of me

50

. . . You like being loved . . . but you're afraid to love
back . . .

Stephen But I'm ready for it . . . Let me . . . I want to
look at you. Now.

Anna You can get me to do anything you want, you
know that.

Stephen Do it.

Anna parts her legs.

Wider . . . The mouth of the world . . .

Anna My mouth.

Stephen Let me hold you a little bit . . .

Anna Don't touch me here . . . I couldn't . . .

Stephen No . . . no . . . Can I ask? Is it too late? Has the
moment passed? Have I made you wait too long, being
indecisive? Sometimes I think people prefer their habits to
their life. I do know what I want now.

He holds and kisses Anna.

Russell (*calls*) Anna!

Anna I'm afraid of being caught. We can't stay here.

Russell (*calls*) Anna!

Anna Just tell me quickly, if you've made up your mind.
What is it you want?

Stephen (*to Anna*) You . . . you . . . you . . . I want hours
and weeks and months and years and years and years of
you.

Anna Now I'm here, I can tell you – you've got to forget
me Stephen. Let's erase one another from our heads and get
on with our lives. It's not so difficult to forget someone –

Stephen If you put your mind to it –

Anna It is possible.

Stephen I know. But there was something valuable and extraordinary between us . . . some love worth pursuing to see where it would take us . . .

Anna Forget about it. Look after yourself . . . (*She goes.*)

Stephen No! No!

End of Act One.

Act Two

SCENE ONE

The summer-house in the garden. The house behind, from which music drifts.

Barry Lorraine . . . What are you doing here?

Lorraine Why shouldn't I be here?

Barry Are you waiting for someone? Or hiding? Did you have to get away from those awful people?

Lorraine I'm just thinking.

Barry I'm bursting out all over. I might explode. I can't wear these one more minute.

Lorraine Get them off then.

Barry I will. Don't think I haven't read my D. H. Lawrence. Are you sure?

Lorraine Go for it.

Barry You just go on thinking while I strip down . . . I can't wear these one more minute . . . It's not me . . . Dry-clean only . . . I've never had anything dry-cleaned in my life. Where's the bloody water I've heard about?

Lorraine Down there. It'll get dark.

Barry Are you coming in?

Lorraine I can't swim.

Barry Oh, can't you?

Lorraine Don't stay in long.

Barry After a certain age you never feel really free . . .

53

There's always a shelf to put up somewhere . . . or some-one to prevent going mad. I need to feel free – (*Naked, he hands her his clothes.*) Don't you fancy a little fishing? I'll undress you. (*Pause.*) Speak to Julie?

Lorraine She wouldn't understand what I was trying to say . . .

Barry As Stalin told us, the undesirable classes aren't going to liquidate themselves.

Lorraine Who?

Barry Say it louder . . . and when she's had a few drinks. (*Pause.*) Meet me later and we'll celebrate. Bring a towel.

Lorraine Your other clothes should be dry now.

Barry Good. Lorraine, if you see Sophie, tell her I'm waiting for her. She can purify herself too! (*He holds her.*) Solidarity! (*He runs towards the water.*) We're all naked underneath! Yes!

She picks up his clothes and walks off with them. Barry sings 'Jerusalem'. At last we hear a splash.

(*off*) Fuck – a cold freedom!

Lorraine Mad, mad, mad. Julie . . .

Stephen and Sophie are in the summer-house.

Sophie . . . Is there a light in here?

Stephen Somewhere. I come here to read and think at night, but usually end up sitting in the dark . . . Hold on . . .

Laughter.

Sophie . . . I'll drop the bottle!

Stephen But it's the most important thing. Give it here –

54

Sophie Stephen –

Stephen I wouldn't recognize you in the dark now. Your old arse has dropped –

Sophie And your stomach hasn't!

Stephen I want to see the grey pubic hairs like everyone else . . . I'll have them out with my new teeth.

Sophie Hold my hand . . . I want to remember how you feel . . . Your skin was like a baby's. Yes. Squeeze me.

Stephen We were children then . . . (*He turns the light on.*) Sophie. Something's happened here this evening and I need to ask you an important favour.

Sophie Give me a drink at least.

Stephen I've never said, but I'm sorry for everything.

Sophie Sorry we got rid of the child?

Stephen I don't know.

> *We see Lorraine – holding Barry's clothes – watching them through the back of the summer-house.*
> *Pause.*

Sophie You persuaded me . . . you were absolutely certain you didn't want it.

Stephen I was with Julie by then.

Sophie He still haunts me, our little boy . . .

Stephen Where are the glasses? (*Pause.*) Why won't you take the job? You don't appear to have scared Russell off. The opposite in fact . . . Wait . . .

Charles (*coming on*) Lorraine!

> *Lorraine bolts from the summer-house and runs into Charles.*

55

Lorraine There you are. I've been – What's the matter? Has the boy woken up?

Charles Does Stephen seem agitated?

Lorraine Why? Because Sophie still loves him?

Charles What? (*Pause.*) No, no . . . Oh, I'm a failure. No, half a failure. Actually, three-quarters more like . . . if I include the children. Bad husband, too. But I want to do something. This film. I wish Stephen would give it to me. The thing is, he works on five things at once, and he's tricky. I can't even be sure he's writing it –

Lorraine He's never missed a day since I worked for them. It's on his desk in their bedroom . . . I take him his coffee and he talks to me about it . . .

Charles How is it?

Lorraine Long and funny and . . . very sad.

Charles That'll have them queuing round the block. What's it called?

Lorraine *Lick the Plate, Nigel.*

Charles Catchy. If you could . . . fetch it for me.

Lorraine Without him knowing?

Charles We'll replace it in a couple of hours. Say it was me. His mind's on other things.

Lorraine I can't do that.

Charles holds her.

Oh, that's nice . . . I've been wanting someone to rub my shoulders . . . You couldn't ask Julie to give me a pay rise – and a holiday . . .

Charles Go and fetch it, sweet little darling . . .

Lorraine You'll be nice to me.

Charles Oh yes. Very.

She goes.

Good, good. I'm not quite the wanker I like to think . . .

Stephen and Sophie in the summer-house.

Stephen Here we are.

Sophie People can't always take care of themselves.
Barry's fragile –

Stephen Cheers!

Sophie If Barry and I are careful, we could make enough
happiness to live on . . . and that would be sufficient . . .

Stephen You are so submissive. No one's watching . . .

Sophie You've become pretty conservative yourself – I can
see you getting more and more shut off . . .

Stephen Listen. It's this. Tomorrow I'm away.

Sophie Where?

Stephen A new life. Almost definitely.

Sophie What are you talking about?

Stephen When Anna walked in and I saw her tonight . . .
for the first time in weeks, it all returned, a world opening
out . . . the unexpected at midnight.

Sophie Is that her? But she's come with him. (*Pause.*) She's
young . . . young for you.

Stephen She'll age. (*Pause.*) What do you really think?
Isn't she –

Sophie Can't we adult women hold conversations?
Couldn't I suck your penis until your soul floated out of

your ears, raise the children as concert pianists and run you three times round the block? Men looked at me all the time . . .

Stephen You would fly across the road and remonstrate with workmen who whistled at you. Now you'd give them money . . . (*Pause.*) I met her by chance –

Sophie You still pick up women – I'd go out of the room at a party and you'd have made a date with someone else. (*Pause.*) We could all go from person to person. Isn't that called the free market? Browse and buy, pick and choose, rent and reject . . . no sexual or social security . . . everyone forced to take care of themselves . . .

Stephen She's a lot to manage. She's petulant and sulky . . . she takes offence . . . She's poor, virtually uneducated . . . Where she's from they put glasses in each others' faces – Yet she has grace. Where does that come from? She adores me –

Sophie Your old prick's her only chance, you fool . . .

Stephen Please. I'm asking if you would speak to her for me . . . She has come with that wretched undertaker –

Sophie Who you sent me to –

Stephen I had no idea it was him she was seeing. Which Crosby, Stills and Nash record was it?

Sophie 'Love the One You're With'.

Pause. They giggle and slap hands.

Stephen Soph . . . Tell her that I'm quite a good man, and that I want her.

Sophie I don't know, Stephen . . . It's a hard thing for me.

Stephen Yes . . . Come on . . . Soph . . .

Sophie Let me think . . .

Stephen Tell her not to give her body to the undertaker tonight.

Sophie Don't you sleep with Julie?

Stephen The years I've paddled in that dispiriting flesh hoping for some recognition . . . It'll be the last paddle . . . and then I'll be free.

We see Anna walking in the garden.

I would lie in this place, all night sometimes . . . wishing for her to walk in . . . not knowing why I was somewhere I didn't want to be . . . unable to understand how it is that people do – repeatedly – things that are not in their best interest . . . and how they manage to keep their appetite, their passion, their love of life alive . . .

Sophie I don't know.

Stephen Didn't I get you a job?

Sophie But it wasn't as a madam. I'll think about it.

Stephen Thanks.

They go off.
Barry runs naked across the stage, dripping wet.

Barry Lorraine . . . Lorraine . . . Oh God . . . I went right under and into the slime. Something went round my ankle . . . I could have had a heart attack . . . There was no one there! I was completely alone! Lorraine – Where are you? Lorraine!

Anna, walking alone, runs into Barry, who is attempting to conceal himself with a leafy branch pulled from a tree.

Barry Help. Oh God. Help . . . if you don't mind . . .

Anna Who is it?

Barry I'm the schoolteacher. Barry. Don't be afraid . . .
Birnham Wood has come to Dunsinane.

Anna What?

Barry Lorraine's got my underwear. She's not wearing it.
She's bringing it from my room.

Anna I was going to try the water.

Barry No. It's more of a whirlpool than a river.

Anna Like this place.

Barry Come on, history will take care of them.

Anna Leave me! I want to go in!

Barry No, no . . . Don't do that, please.

He holds her. Charles comes on.

Charles What a lovely penis.

Barry Where's Lorraine?

Charles Are you sure she'll be interested? (*to Anna*)
Anna. (*to Barry*) She's gone to fetch something. I'll get
Sophie –

Barry Not when I'm like this! I hope Lorraine hurries . . .

Charles Lorraine has never hurried . . . I hope you
haven't requested anything that isn't on her job descrip-
tion . . .

Barry What about trousers?

Charles Trousers? Trousers . . . I don't think so. I doubt
it. (*Pause.*) Just relax. They say teaching's a severe pro-
fession . . . Are you a follower of Rousseau? (*to Anna*)
You . . .

Anna Charles . . . please tell me how to get to the main
road. I'm going to hitch back to London . . . I didn't real-

ize it was all so idyllic . . . and Julie was only a name to me . . .

Charles What about the under– Russell, I mean?

Anna I don't want to spoil it for him either. My mind has gone a bit mad . . .

Charles Recently I was on my knees barking like a dog myself . . . But I want to say, Stephen –

Anna Yes? . . .

Charles He –

Lorraine comes on with something under her jumper.

Lorraine Look what I've got up me jumper.

Charles You're a delightful little wobbling minx.

Barry Terrific –

Charles kisses her and looks at the manuscript. Barry tries to snatch it.

What's this?

Charles A film. Don't wet it –

Barry Where's my clothes?

Lorraine Clothes?

Barry My strides!

Lorraine I forgot!

Barry Forgot! I could die! (*to Charles*) Give me that! A couple of pages would do –

Charles Maybe a paragraph, but no!

Anna Here. Take this. (*She gives Barry a long cardigan.*)

Barry Thanks, thanks. You're kind. I wanted to be free.

Anna That's okay.

Barry puts the cardigan on.

Charles I'll put this somewhere safe until later tonight . . . Then I'll know . . . (*to Anna*) Have you read much of Stephen's stuff?

Anna I saw one of his films on television, by accident. I know he's written some other stories and a novel . . . I saw him read to an audience once . . . But I didn't like all the other people looking at him . . . I'll get my things.

Charles Wait – I know you need to go but there are things that need to be discussed.

Anna I think I should get out of here.

Charles In a bit.

Barry takes Lorraine to one side.

Barry Please – Go and get . . . my trousers and things.

Lorraine I asked Julie what you said.

Barry touches her.

No – The guests often think I come with the room –

Barry I'm only trying to keep warm. Solidarity, it's called. You're brave. It's only the beginning –

Lorraine She sacked me. I'm out on Monday. I've lost my home!

Barry Stay with us. I'll have to ask Sophie, of course –

Lorraine Where d'you holiday?

Barry We move around.

Lorraine Oh yes?

Barry In a camper van.

Lorraine A camper van?

Barry A Volkswagen. Just honest working people. Not like –

Lorraine I don't want a fucking camper van. Julie knows things, and she's hard, with a rich husband. The other nannies . . . They're easily satisfied . . . I never want to be poor . . .

Barry I'll sort it out . . . once I've got clothes.

Lorraine Running around with trousers isn't my job. You'll be cold. I'll light the fire in your room –

Barry Please . . .

Lorraine Anything for the weekend?

Barry What?

Lorraine You don't want to buy any cocaine, do you? I'm not a dealer. It's just that I've lost my job.

As Barry follows her off, Sophie comes on.

Barry (*to Sophie*) It's not a dress!

Sophie (*to Barry*) They won't ask us again.

Barry (*to Sophie*) I've got snails under my arms, and pains. I can't breathe.

Lorraine So what d'you think I should do now . . .

Barry I'll tell you. But first, stand in front of me. (*He goes off with Lorraine.*)

Sophie Anna –

Anna Yes –

Charles Don't let her go.

Pause. Charles moves away.

Anna You know Stephen well.

Sophie He told you . . .

Anna I can't find my way around London yet. We walked about for days. He showed me the flat you lived in as students . . .

Sophie He did? I've known Russell too . . . for as long. Isn't he good company?

Anna . . . Sometimes, because I'm not with Stephen . . . sometimes I just break down and can't go out. I keep his answering machine messages and play them. Is that what love is?

Sophie Initially. Was it Plato, or Diana Ross, who said love isn't in the beloved, but in the one who loves? How did you meet Stephen?

Anna I went to see Charles for a job. Once, girls dreamed of being ballerinas. Now they want to be on television. Stephen was sitting in his office with his feet on the table. He put them down when I walked in. Of course, I was just fluff . . . But he kept on being interested. He's not some unformed boy, though. His past, who he is, the children . . . his work . . . his moods . . .

Sophie You know about Julie and the children?

Anna He never lied. I just didn't know what it all meant. When he sits there thinking and just ignores you. It's a whole life . . . He'll swallow me up and I'll never escape . . . My father went away when I was young. After, my mother's men were . . . disappointing. I've never had a man for myself before, except with me, in my mind, all the time. But women pay Stephen attention . . . they want to talk to him . . . I won't share him . . . I would have to . . . wouldn't I?

Sophie You do that now.

64

Anna I never know what I'm doing . . . but when he talks to me . . . he makes me feel that everything is all right . . . he's learned how to take care of a woman . . .

Sophie At last. (*Pause.*) I thought women of your generation had contempt for men.

Anna If we do, it's only because we need them so much.

Sophie But Stephen tires of women . . .

Anna Is that what happened to you?

Sophie Julie's intelligent . . . bookish . . . She can earn money. They like to talk . . .

Anna Yes. (*Pause.*) I'm young . . . men like me. I'm better off with Russell, until I get over Stephen . . . aren't I? Russell asked me to marry him.

Sophie He did? Well, why not?

Anna Yes. (*Pause.*) Please . . . I know Stephen likes to see you.

Sophie Did he say that?

Anna I want to know . . . Does Stephen mention me sometimes?

Sophie Yeah.

Pause.

Anna A lot?

Pause.

Sophie Enough.

Pause.

Anna I don't think I can wait any more. I should forget the whole thing.

Sophie I think so.

Anna It'll take a while . . . but it happens, doesn't it. Is that what you did? Is that how you forgot him?

Sophie Yes.

Anna And you're happy now . . . and everything's all right? That's your boyfriend, the . . . large man – I don't mean –

Sophie Yes . . .

Anna Oh God, I've lost my ear-ring . . . I had it just now . . . I can't go without it – I just won't! It's special . . . Sophie, thanks. Will you help me look . . .

Sophie Come on.

They go.

SCENE TWO

In the summer-house, Stephen is cutting up cocaine. Russell with him.

Russell Years ago, Julie and I worked together on a game show. *Jack's Pot.* We'd spend the day shopping for the prizes. Then we'd go to Doreen's to do the questions and gossip. I know her well, and she gets a little belligerent, but now she seems discouraged and bewildered . . .

Stephen Poor Julie . . .

Russell They're all coming apart . . . attacking one another . . . affairs and heartbreak – most of the people I know. No one knows how to make themselves or anyone else happy. Marriage hardly seems worth the trouble . . .

Stephen What else is there?

66

Russell Money. Work –

Stephen Russell, I wanted to say . . . I'm pleased you're helping Sophie –

Russell I used to think . . . you know, when she was with you . . . that she was dazzling . . . For some reason she never left my mind.

Stephen Nor mine.

Russell I was shocked, when you sent her to see me, by how little she'd done with herself –

Stephen If you can say that about anyone else's life. I prefer the long way round myself – that way you see more.

Russell You? I've never met anyone more ambitious.

Stephen Only in my work, not in love . . . until . . . Perhaps you should spend more time getting to know the girl. Anna. Is that her name?

Russell I never get too attached. I've got too –

Stephen Tell me one thing you – that interests you about her.

Russell I forgot you like these little games. One thing? She's got this –

Stephen Don't! Sorry.

Russell What? I was going to say, she's got someone else . . . Who messes her about.

Stephen Does she talk about him? Is he kind to her?

Russell I'll go and ask her.

Stephen indicates the cocaine.

I can't . . . I'm a public figure. Minor, of course –

Stephen Set a good example –

Russell And I have to go to bed with Anna . . . I want to be on good form. It's distressing, the thought of that young flesh waiting for me . . . But Julie, do you think –

Stephen Lick it up.

Russell Eh?

Stephen gets hold of Russell.

What are you doing? You can't hold me like that . . .

Stephen You're not in some smart restaurant now – I might rip your eyes out and stuff them up your narrow little arse –

Russell No thanks –

Stephen . . . On behalf of the public, mind, for those vet programmes!

Charles comes on. Stephen shoves Russell's face down into the coke.

Russell Fuck, what the fuck –

Stephen Yeah!

Charles If he doesn't want any there's more for us –

Russell Christ!

Stephen Get down, rat-face!

Charles Look at him!

Barry comes on to see Stephen spitting in his hand and wiping the coke across Russell's face.

Russell God!

Charles What a waste. Wait . . . just there . . . in the eye-brows – (*He removes some coke from Russell's eyebrow and transfers it to his nose.*)

Russell (*to Stephen*) You always were arrogant –

Stephen Now I'm going to beat him like a dog.

Barry (*restraining Stephen*) . . . And I thought the conversation here would be too intellectual for me!

Russell (*to Stephen*) Stephen . . . I'm not crazy about you . . . but I respect you . . . (*to Charles*) Is it the drugs that make him mad?

Charles (*to Russell*) We haven't had any yet. Let me brush you down.

Barry Stephen . . . why has Lorraine been sacked?

Charles Then I'm going to relax. Dear, oh dear –

Stephen Has she?

Charles For what?

Stephen The girl has been losing the will to live. All nannies, like all teachers, do, after a time. It's when you hear the words 'sick', 'headache' that you know.

Barry You can't just throw people away when –

Stephen Everything you believe I abhor, so don't come it with me.

Barry You made speeches and wrote –

Stephen The attempt to crush individuality, the imagination . . . wit, originality . . . What men and women make is the only interesting thing and nothing but death was made by all that Marxism.

Barry Well, you've said it then. There isn't much of 'interest' if you work in a factory in the Third World. You haven't always been a dirty snob. Young people, and working people, were inspired by your writing.

Stephen The upper middle classes are the carriers of culture, of the extended and stretched human mind . . . of what we can be and do which isn't just menial. It's the erotic anarchy of the imagination I like. All the great works and ideas have it. Along with something strange. But your revolutions kill the people who do the thinking and imagining because you can't bear the differences between people – That is a bit dim, isn't it?

Barry People in the art line take themselves very seriously –

Russell Give me a magician with a three-legged dog –

Stephen Nuts for monkeys –

Barry – Thinking they can be excluded from the values which apply to everyone else. Anyone but me would call that fucking arrogant.

Charles Barry . . . Think how consoling it would be, while you're waiting for a bus, or teaching – to know you have achieved something. That Stephen can take an incident, part of a person, and say something about how we live . . . Don't you think – how does he do it?

Barry I never think that –

Charles Talent, fulfilled talent, is an ultimate value, the only lasting, irreducible thing and it's unevenly distributed, like beauty –

Barry Everyone has a spark of imagination . . . but no one believes in them. (*to Stephen*) You're not exactly the guy who made *Bicycle Thieves*, are you . . . Your work might improve if you came to my school. Sophie says you're not concerned with anything outside yourself.

Stephen Sophie . . . I am interested by my own mind – because I am like everyone else.

Barry That's a lie. You're rich. A street cleaner is more

70

useful than you, and should be paid more.

Stephen (*indicating Russell*) Why slander a scribbler when – I know it's hard to believe but indulge me a moment – he's one of the most influential people in the country?

Russell It is a mercy that I have no desire to influence people . . . What I want . . . is entertainment, distraction . . . none of your profundity saved a single soul this century. In fact it turned on the gas.

Stephen It's a force, banality . . . a kind of tyranny . . . Why not strive?

Russell I went out and got all of Mahler's records and I've seen *The Magic Flute* twice.

Stephen Listen. We were in Venice. I tossed Lorraine's dark glasses in the Grand Canal –

Russell – But I preferred the rubbish. It was always funnier and done better . . .

Stephen I said to Lorraine, 'Open your eyes – look, look, there is this too!' The depth of that which there is to draw on – European civilization since the Renaissance, despite its lapses, encouraged by Barry – to sustain us, is limitless. It would be foolish to be too modest about this, or too haughty . . . but some recognition of where we have arrived might be an idea . . . otherwise we are dealing unnecessarily in trinkets rather than gold . . . Why do you have such a low idea of what people are capable of understanding . . .?

Barry Yes, that's it . . . it's low . . .

Stephen . . . Banal, repetitive, formulaic, without invention or –

Russell Not everyone is at your pompous level. Fifty

years ago I'd have been running a music hall. Now that's glamour – one man and a glove puppet –

Barry I'm teaching in a hut –

Russell A hut?

Barry Not a mud hut – but a hut in a London school. When it rains we have to send the pupils home. You'd think people would consider education important . . . If you would, just once, leave your small name-dropping, arse-kissing world –

Russell All right, I will. I'll come and see, after Boston . . .

Barry It seems a strange thing to say . . . but what I do in the school – is try and like them –

Russell You don't impart any information at all?

Barry All that follows . . .

Russell Good night . . . (*to Stephen*) You –

Stephen 'Love the one you're with' . . .

Russell goes. Charles follows him.

Charles (*to Russell*) . . . None of it went in your eye, I hope . . . Do you want me to blow it out?

Russell No, thank you . . .

Barry (*to Stephen*) I can't believe it wasn't a good idea . . . equality . . . not exploiting people . . . fraternity . . . seeing the excluded as human . . . (*Pause.*) Russell's offered Sophie this job . . . Does he mean it?

Stephen Yes.

Barry Should I let her do it . . .? I want to let her go . . . freedom, you know. I don't know what to do . . . I'm afraid of losing her into another world . . .

72

Stephen Have a drink . . . Don't worry . . . Why are you asking me?

Barry Being a writer, I thought you might . . .

Stephen No . . . no idea about anything . . . None at all . . .

SCENE THREE

Charles is settling down to read the manuscript. Lorraine comes on.

Lorraine It doesn't matter to you . . . but I'm out of work –

Charles You're not.

Lorraine Have you fixed it?

Charles kisses her. She responds.

Charles You like me a little bit? I'm surprised . . . I've got no money at all, I'm ashamed to say . . .

Lorraine . . . Would you . . . Sometimes men ask, what do you like, as if you'd volunteer to be whipped. I like to be stroked –

Charles Somehow I've got children but I can't say I know how to touch a woman –

Lorraine You need practise.

Charles You think I might benefit?

Lorraine I'll put this behind my head and you just benefit away – (*Pause.*) Did you know you've got hairs growing out of the end of your nose? You get chocolate round your mouth . . . I watch you eating . . .

Charles You look at me.

73

Lorraine Let your hands go where they want . . .

Charles That's an invitation I've waited years for. (*He strokes and massages her.*) All I want is to feel I can do things differently . . . That I'm not a rat on a wheel . . . I want to be reincarnated without actually dying . . . if you see what I mean . . .

Lorraine Pull my hair –

Charles . . . And know whether I can have what everyone else has . . . a little love, children who speak to me now and again, a woman's loving arms . . . some honest contact three times a day.

Lorraine Yes . . . Dig into me . . .

Charles Is that too much?

Lorraine No . . . no . . . no . . . Tell me more . . . The things you talk about . . . I like to hear them . . .

Charles Well . . . I was sent away to school at seven. That's what they did then . . . and . . . Shall I undo this pretty little button?

Lorraine Oh, Charles. It would be wonderful if you did that. But I might lose my job. Let's go back there. Inside!

Barry joins Sophie, Anna and Russell.

Russell (*to Anna*) . . . Where were you?

Anna I don't know . . .

Russell You don't know . . . It's annoying, the way you make me look for you . . .

Sophie (*to Barry*) She lost her ear-ring.

Russell Right. Do you want me to help?

Anna That would be nice.

74

They look for it.

Russell (*to Anna*) You don't know Stephen, but he's pretty mad.

Anna He is?

Russell He turned on me. Just now. Without warning.

Anna Were you talking about the ratings? What was it about?

Russell I don't know –

Anna You didn't hurt him, did you?

Russell Hurt him?

Anna Don't you like him being like that? Sometimes I wish I weren't sensible . . .

Russell (*to Anna*) Stephen's sinister. He's always on the look-out for women. Years ago, Sophie worshipped him, and he threw her away. He regrets it.

Anna He said that? (*Pause.*) Or did she say that – did she?

Russell It isn't of any interest to you anyway. Let's look for this ear-ring and get to bed.

They drift away.

Barry (*to Sophie*) I've thought . . . that I don't want you to work with him . . . Sophie –

Sophie (*to Barry*) No . . . I know that . . .

Barry I'm absolutely against it . . . You see what I mean . . . I'll tell him if you want. I think I will. You haven't spoken to him about it?

Sophie I will now. (*Pause.*) You know, Stephen is leaving Julie. He's off.

Barry Is he?

75

Sophie For a girl.

Barry The courage. The cowardice. Fuck. How unkind. Does she know? (*Pause.*) He'll buy another place. The children will stay with him. Separation is a luxury the rich can afford. We're stuck with one another.

Sophie Do you mind if I make a joint? It's the only thing that grows in our garden.

> *She starts smoking a joint. Julie comes out with Anna, Russell following.*

Russell Anna's lost an ear-ring.

Julie I'll help you look . . . in a minute.

Barry Julie . . .

Julie So you were sucked under.

> *The sound of Charles and Lorraine making love.*

Barry I was, yes.

Julie It's a fast river. Are you enjoying it here, otherwise?

Barry Yes. And you seem relaxed. I wanted to say, Julie . . . about Lorraine . . .

> *The sound of the love-making increases.*

Julie Yes?

Barry She never has a minute to herself. She never stops. You could, you know, give her a bit more . . . a rise, you know.

> *Everyone listens and laughs.*

I think it might rain. (*Pause. To Russell*) Drink?

Russell Yes, thanks. God, yes.

> *Russell and Barry sit down together.*

76

Barry He gave you a scare . . . eh? Tell me –

Russell Yes?

Barry When you sit down to relax at the end of a day's work, why is there never anything good on the telly?

Russell Let me think about that.

Julie (*to Sophie*) Sean coughs all night . . . phlegm and spew. Sometimes I think he's going to explode . . . Thanks. (*She takes the joint.*)

Sophie We had that with both of them . . . for a month.

Julie There's not much you can do.

Sophie Except sit there with them in the middle of the night, in the dark and cold, wondering –

Julie How did it, so suddenly, when you weren't looking –

Sophie One day you were dancing in your bedroom –

Julie Worrying about your skin –

Anna Yes . . .

Sophie Men don't lose their youth overnight . . . I remember the night mine departed . . . out of the window, like Peter Pan . . . cheerio . . .

Julie Still, you've got yourself a job, I believe.

Sophie But I'm afraid that I can't do it . . . Men don't feel guilty about the children the way women do. Well – Charles does. Stephen would.

Julie Why should he?

Anna I'm like that . . . afraid . . .

Sophie Afraid the other people will be too quick and sophisticated for us . . .

Anna Is it just women that are like that?

Sophie (*to Julie*) You're not like that.

Julie I know I'm better – or not worse . . .

Anna Do you?

Sophie But are such things worth wanting? When you wake up in the morning, what do you really want to do?

Anna Exactly –

Sophie I didn't believe, twenty years ago, that we were freeing women so they could rush on to the tube and sit in an office for twelve hours. We imagined more creative freedoms. That somehow we would live like artists . . . (*Pause.*) Still, Barry's a good husband. He'll do anything. That's why I chose him.

Julie You did?

Sophie Yes, partly, though I've never admitted it. (*Pause.*) Does Stephen get up for the children?

Julie Stephen would never get up for anyone but himself . . .

Anna (*taking the joint from Sophie*) It's not a good idea to get too dependent on a man is it? (*Pause.*) Does love last? You don't want too much . . . or too little, do you. (*Pause.*) Does it go on . . . or all come down in pettiness and bickering . . .

Julie . . . That is something a young woman would like to know . . .

Sophie There's always pettiness . . . but there has to be something more, to make it worth bearing . . .

Anna I know what I'm going to do: walk out of the house and travel until I forget all this . . . going anywhere I feel like . . . Africa, Tibet, Iceland . . .

Sophie Yes . . . That'll pass the time.

Anna But?

Sophie In the end you'll have to see whether you can do it.

Anna What?

Sophie Go into a room with someone you hardly know and see if you can get on with them for the rest of your life.

Julie What's that? There. Your ear-ring.

Anna Oh God, thank you, Julie.

Sophie That's good.

Julie It's pretty.

Anna (*to Julie*) You must be proud of Stephen, Julie. Of everything that he's done . . . Of what he is.

Julie (*looking at the ear-ring*) I've got a similar pair.

Russell (*to Anna*) We could go upstairs now.

Julie I love going to bed.

Sophie Yes, I used to see it as the high point of the day. But, like my children, I'm rebelling . . . another day gone . . . I'm not standing for sleep . . . another day gone . . . no . . . no . . . Who's having another drink?

Julie Me, please. (*to Sophie*) I used to forget Stephen for days . . . Then, suddenly, he'd be there . . . blazing in my face and we'd be one thing again . . . But now I worry about him constantly . . . as if I don't know how to satisfy him . . . I really must talk to him . . .

Barry goes across as Julie starts to go.

We've made mistakes . . . but it's not too late, I know it isn't . . . Anna's right. It's never too late to tell people that you love them. Where is he?

79

She goes. Sophie puts the music on. Barry comes up behind her and kisses her neck and shoulders.

Barry All I want is to feel you and be with you . . . Come on . . .

They dance in a desultory sort of way, then stop.

Russell (*to Anna*) What is the matter?

Stephen comes on.

Anna I'm restless. I won't be able to sleep . . .

Russell Why did you come?

Anna Just to see.

Russell Are you thinking of him?

Anna I always think of him.

Russell I like you, really.

Anna Do you? You don't know me.

Russell I want to. Do you want some wine? Here. There's a little left. Get it down you. Go on . . .

Stephen Leave her.

Russell You –

Anna It's found . . .

She holds out the ear-ring. Russell kisses her.

Sophie Stephen, Julie's looking for you.

Stephen Is she?

Russell Do you love this man you're always thinking of?

Anna I'm trying not to.

Russell What is he? Some kind of rich guy?

Stephen (*to Russell*) May I dance with your girlfriend?

Russell If she wants to.

Stephen How about it?

Anna I can't say no.

Stephen Don't then.

Anna What sort of dance do you want to do?

Stephen Something that goes on a long time.

Anna Have you got the stamina?

Stephen If you hold me up.

Stephen and Anna dance.

Barry They look like a happy couple.

Russell Don't they? (*Pause.*) Sophie?

Barry It must be because they don't know one another –

Sophie and Russell dance. Lorraine walks across with a duvet.

Stephen (*to Anna*) I want to tell you something . . .

Anna What is it?

He whispers in her ear. She laughs.

Russell (*to Sophie*) Have you thought about everything –

Sophie Yes, I have . . .

Russell And so . . .

Charles is dressing Lorraine in the summer-house.

Charles (*to Lorraine*) . . . Do you do much of it?

Lorraine I had a soldier on the train on the way down.

Charles I suppose sex is a good way of meeting people.

Lorraine That's it . . .

Charles I think I might read now. (*Pause.*) Thank you . . . for the greatest moment of my life.

Lorraine Don't be grateful . . .

Charles What?

Lorraine You're good too . . . The things you said . . . were all right . . .

Charles Were they . . .

Lorraine They gave me confidence. You're a decent man.

Charles Thank you.

Lorraine Kiss me, then.

Charles Right.

Lorraine (*to Barry*) Have you spoken to Julie?

Barry It's difficult . . . I started to –

Lorraine I've got to do the beds . . . but it's not really my job.

Barry Don't do it then.

Everybody dances. Lorraine watches.

(*to Lorraine, asking her to dance*) How about it?

Lorraine Yes . . .

SCENE FOUR

Later. Charles is reading. Julie comes in.

Julie Something interesting? It must have been to drag you away from Lorraine.

Charles Ah, Julie – It was a lovely supper.

Julie Did Stephen give this to you? He said he wasn't going to . . .

Charles Why?

Julie Your life is bleak and neglected.

Charles Sorry? (*Pause.*) Is that right?

Julie He tries to help you, but you depress him. Talking to you is like sitting in a draught. Show it to me.

Charles I can't. Wait.

Julie (*taking it*) What's it about?

Charles The usual things –

Julie What are they?

Charles A man meets a woman and –

Julie Which woman?

Charles Oh, it's all made up –

Julie He can't make things up.

Charles Don't – Julie . . . What's wrong? What are you doing?

Julie Why should everyone but me read it? It's not that I'm interested . . . It's the only way I can know what he's thinking . . . He used to show me his work. I would sit beside him at his desk for hours and days on end . . . We did it together . . . I made him work hard . . . he didn't believe in himself . . .

Charles You told him he was becoming self-important, that he was mediocre and understood nothing of others . . . You –

Julie He said that? (*Pause.*) The children came. I didn't sleep. I couldn't think about him the whole time!

Charles follows Julie around.

Where is he?

Charles How do I know?

Julie You usually do. You've got no talent . . . no ability at anything . . . except as a parasite. Why d'you always have to be telephoning, or hanging around here like a lap-dog?

Charles I'm his friend.

Julie His servant more like –

Charles Jealousy is a terrible devil. Actually, he's dancing –

Julie With her?

Charles Yes.

Julie He doesn't dance. What does it matter if he dances with Sophie. (*Pause.*) You and Stephen have conspired against me, I know that. (*She holds the script out.*) I'll give it back to you, but tell me something.

Charles Okay . . .

Julie Does he love me? (*Pause.*) So. I won't ask again. I understand everything. Yes. Oh well . . . There it is. Done for. Oh dear . . . He's too afraid to admit that he doesn't . . .

Charles Julie –

Julie Do you know what the funny thing is? I've always known it . . . I just didn't believe it.

Charles You thought he would come round?

Julie I thought there was enough to get by on . . . just enough . . . to sustain a life . . . together . . .

Sophie and Barry come across.

Charles (*to Julie*) Give me that. Come on . . . Stephen'll go crazy.

Julie (*to Charles*) I'll punch you in the face if you come near me . . . (*She goes off with the manuscript.*) Thank you for this . . . Thank you very much . . .

Sophie (*to Charles*) Want a drink?

Charles Yes, comrade, I think I do. Thank you. Oh God . . . I'm so old. I was young for ages . . . and then suddenly . . .

Barry I think I'll talk properly to Julie about Lorraine. Is it a good time, do you think?

Charles Oh yes. It's always a good time to provoke the middle classes, don't you think?

Sophie (*to Barry*) Go on. And I'll talk to Russell then . . .

Barry He won't try and persuade you to work with him?

Sophie I couldn't have done it anyway . . . I'm too far from that world.

Barry We're a family. (*Pause.*) Sophie . . . Can I ask you? He's never tried to touch you, has he?

Sophie Russell? Russell.

Barry No, no . . . You wouldn't . . . sorry . . .

Sophie No, no, I don't think I would . . .

Barry Right. (*Pause.*) Julie . . . Julie . . .

He goes off after Julie.

Charles (*to Sophie*) Julie's stolen Stephen's script and

85

she's reading it. She's spitting needles, and I let her grab it
. . . by mistake . . . (*Pause.*) What's the thing you most
fear? Do you know? For me it's being disliked . . . not
having my love returned . . . You?

Sophie I wake up and I have to rack my brains to think
of a reason to continue. I'm sick of feeling bad most of
the time. I'm going, now, to rebel against my own mind.
Rebel against living with the idea that everything has to
be poisoned by fear and hopelessness. It has kept me
down. I know how much of this there is around . . . and I
know I can't just banish it but I'm going to be aware of
how it goes . . . and fight . . . fight . . . being sickened by
myself . . . I want activity . . . vigour . . . life . . .

Russell and Anna come in.

Russell (*to Anna*) Shall we take a bottle and get upstairs?

Anna Can't we have a drink here?

Russell Resistance is exciting, as I was only saying to
someone at Disney the other day –

Sophie Russell . . . Barry and I have discussed it and we
thought . . .

Russell Good. See you in the office.

Sophie When?

Russell Monday. You know where it is.

Sophie Yes. I'll be there. Right? Why not? (*to Anna*)
Listen . . .

Russell (*to Anna*) Red, white or pink?

Sophie (*whispers to Anna*) He loves you. Stephen . . .

Anna (*to Sophie*) What?

Russell Anna . . .

Anna Please say it again . . . I didn't quite . . .

Sophie (*to Anna*) Yes, you did. But you mustn't . . . don't give your body to the undertaker . . . Definitely not.

Anna Right, right. Won't he be with his wife?

Sophie No. (*She goes to Russell.*) Thank you. Thanks . . . for the opportunity. I feel I haven't been gracious enough.

Russell (*to Sophie*) Don't be. I'm really pleased . . . Good . . . good . . .

Sophie Tell me more about it. Will I have to work in the evenings?

Russell Full-time job, love.

Sophie The children –

Russell Not my problem.

Charles (*to Anna*) He's leaving . . . tomorrow, I think. He'll be at my place . . . Will you come there?

Sophie (*to Charles*) I'm going to America again . . .

Russell You'll be brilliant. (*He kisses her. To Anna*) Come on, darling . . . Bring the wine upstairs. Apparently there's a wonderful view from our window . . . You can see Shropshire.

Anna It's dark!

Stephen comes in.
   Barry comes in with Lorraine.

Barry (*to Lorraine*) I've had a word with her.

Lorraine You didn't?

Barry She was reading . . . But she looked up. She even listened. Then she agreed. Oh yes, I've sorted it out for you . . .

Lorraine Excellent . . . You didn't mention the holiday . . .

Barry What? Not my job . . .

Russell We're celebrating . . .

Barry Lovely? What is it?

Sophie Oh, let's leave all that . . .

Russell Sophie and I . . . we're a team . . .

Barry Sorry?

Stephen Good. Good. (*He kisses Sophie.*)

Russell Good night. Sleep well. (*to Anna*) Come on, sweetheart – let yourself go. We'll really be able to relax up there.

Stephen (*to Charles*) If she goes with him . . . I'll remove what's left of your manhood.

Charles What am I supposed to do? I'm a producer, not a hit-man.

Stephen Produce an initiative.

Russell (*to Anna*) You must be quite tired.

Anna Yes, yes I am.

Russell These relaxing weekends can be exhausting. Still . . . once we lie down . . . near one another . . . in a minute.

Anna and Russell go.

Charles (*to Anna and Russell*) Wait – About that script. I'm ready for my pitch.

Russell turns and looks at Charles.

Would you like to . . . er . . .

Russell No, thank you.

Stephen watches them go.

Sophie (*to Stephen*) Sorry.

Stephen Yeah.

Sophie (*to Barry*) Let's go and sleep by the river . . .

Barry Sophie . . .

Sophie It's done and there's no going back . . . I'm going to drink this!

Barry I'll stand and watch.

Stephen (*to Charles*) How was Lorraine?

Charles They're delicious at that age.

Stephen She likes you.

Charles Why? Do you think she'll do it with me again? Twice in one day – it's enough to make an optimist of a misogynist. Want to hear the details? The movement of lips on skin –

Stephen Desire makes me laugh. It makes fools of us all.

Charles Still, rather a fool than a corpse.

Stephen Any day.

Charles Come on. First I said to her . . . just let me undo this recalcitrant little button . . .

Stephen What did she say?

Charles How are you spelling recalcitrant . . . Beginning with an 'f', I said . . .

He takes the despondent Stephen into the summer-house.

Barry (*to Sophie*) You haven't been honest with me . . . I know you haven't . . . Why can't people be straight with one another?

Sophie What do you think of the girl?

Barry She's peculiar . . . I'm not making any progress, you'll be sad to hear . . . But I have got her reinstated . . . with a pay rise. Aren't you jealous? If I thought that you –

Sophie Not the nanny. The other, beautiful, one . . . Does she seem to have any remarkable qualities . . .?

Barry I can't imagine anyone better than you. (*Pause.*) I'm not surprised he gave you that job . . .

Sophie looks at him

Sophie What is it?

Barry I'm not a fool. I've been waiting for you to tell me yourself. Why didn't you? He touched the parts of you I thought were mine. He kissed you. He put his hand between your legs. You touched him. You put him inside you. (*Pause.*) It's easy to destroy a love, like a child hitting a spider's web with a stick . . . didn't you think of that?

Sophie It's not destroyed.

Barry Yes! You've just wiped me out. My confidence, my pride . . .

Sophie More life! That's what I wanted . . . More of everything! That's all it was!

Barry Oh, you vile whore!

Sophie We're together. I'm with you. We'll come through, just about. Only . . . we've got to change. Both of us. We can't be everything to one another. We want to change society but we can't give up our deepest habits of mind. We've got to let ourselves develop. Do you want to do that? Do you think we can do that?

They go off.
Julie walks across the garden with the manuscript.

Charles sees her.

Charles Stephen . . . Stephen.

Stephen Is it now? Let it not be now.

Charles I think so. I think I'll finish my letter to the eldest boy. I write every week. He never replies . . . Perhaps his mother doesn't let him. She will poison him against me, I'm sure. I can survive his hating me as long as he understands that I didn't let him down . . . That it wasn't him I left . . . (*He goes.*)

Julie Would you like me to go into the summer-house?

Stephen What for? No . . . I don't mind holding on to you . . . a bit . . .

Julie Thank you. You know, I have never, ever said that I never loved you.

Stephen Julie . . .

Julie Yes?

Stephen I've arranged to go and stay at Charles's place for a while.

Julie And get the script finalized? Good. You can't work here like it is . . . I'll get the work done while you're away.

Stephen It'll be a while.

Pause.

Julie Where is the love in you, where has it gone . . .? You used to be so tender. How we kissed! (*Pause.*) What will you take? You won't know. Let's pack a bag –

Stephen Thank you, but –

Julie You can't do anything yourself . . . You always ask me to pack for you. Still, you could always come back for other things . . . Have you kissed Sean and Joe . . .?

91

Stephen Joe's not here . . .

Julie tries to hold him, kiss him, touch him.

Julie – Stop it.

Julie Earlier . . . you wanted me to . . . (*Pause.*) You said, last night in bed, the time and passion you've wasted on me. The house, the children, all we have . . . and you've been patronizing me all this time. But why? I don't understand.

Stephen We've been blind, Julie. Why couldn't we recognize before that it was no good . . .!

Anna comes on.

Julie No, no . . . I won't accept that version of things . . . it's a lie – There was good –

Anna Sorry . . . sorry . . .

Stephen What is it?

Anna I wanted . . . something. Milk, I think. Where is the kitchen?

Stephen There might be some on the table . . . I'll get it.

Julie Has the baby woken up? Is he disturbing you?

Anna No. I haven't been to sleep. Or even to bed.

Stephen No?

Julie You've been dancing, I hear. Was it fun?

Anna Stephen dances well.

Julie Does he? Stephen?

Stephen Here . . . It's over-full.

Anna Sorry . . .

Stephen Don't spill it.

He drinks from it. She drinks from it.

Anna Thank you, Stephen, very much.

Stephen That's all right.

Anna goes.

Julie They say . . . I hear . . . people are keen to tell me . . . you go with other women.

Stephen There is someone who likes me.

Julie You? Why would they? (*Pause.*) Sean's been coughing. I keep thinking he's going to choke. What will I do at night without you! They're babies! Don't go . . . Stephen, I can't look after them on my own . . .

Stephen I'll go to Sean now . . .

Julie You can't . . .

Stephen Sorry?

Julie You can keep away, you take drugs, you've got no discipline over the children. He's mine. They're both mine. You want nothing of me, you'll have nothing. I wanted to say . . .

Stephen Yes?

She hits him.

Stephen Christ!

Julie You hurt me!

Stephen Julie –

She hits him again.

Julie We were going to be together! You said so! (*She goes to hit him.*)

Stephen Don't do that! Stop it, stop it, stop, stop, stop!

Julie You'll have nothing! Not the children, not the house, nothing!

Stephen Go to hell! If only you knew how much you bored me!

Julie I hate you!

Lorraine rushes on.

Lorraine (*to Julie*) Stop it now, stop it! All right, all right . . . Let's calm down! Everyone! (*to Stephen*) What are you doing?

Stephen I don't know.

Lorraine I'll take her inside.

Stephen Yes.

Lorraine Come on . . .

Julie I'm not going in – I made the house for him!

Lorraine Sean's crying for you . . .

Julie Right . . . I see.

Lorraine It's okay . . . we'll have a drink and talk about things . . .

She takes Julie off.
Charles comes out of the shadows and goes to Stephen.

Charles We're in trouble.

Stephen It's the children.

Charles It always is. There's a lot of harm done in their name.

Stephen I stayed and stayed and stayed, always hoping, somehow, that over time she would turn into someone else. Is this a common error?

Charles Er . . . yes.

Stephen Oh, my friend, what have I done?

Anna runs across with her bag.

Charles There you are . . . (*to Stephen*) What do you want her to do?

Stephen Ask her.

Charles You must.

Stephen Yes. (*He goes to Anna.*) Be with me, be with me.

Anna I don't know why I want to . . . but I want to.

Stephen I can't say we won't kill each other . . . But it'll be alive. Every day, it'll be alive.

Anna I love you.

Charles Here. (*He throws her his car keys.*) It's the Peugeot. Go. We'll see you Monday.

Anna Yes. Yes. (*She goes.*)

Stephen (*to Charles*) Thank you, friend. Now we'll see . . .

Charles I took your script. You said there's only one subject, what is it to be a human being, living with other people . . . It's there . . . it's present . . . there's life and what's worthwhile . . .

Stephen Will it make money? It gets more and more expensive, breathing every day . . . You only have to kiss someone to start thinking of what it'll cost to divorce them.

Charles I've had a lot of you, these past four years, Stephen . . . The hours of our conversation, in bars and over dinner, saying everything . . . I've never had such a friendship. If you died, my life would be –

Stephen I'm still around . . .

Charles She will have you now . . .

Stephen There's always someone left out. But there's enough love to go round. Oh yes. We'll do the film together . . . that's what I want . . . with you . . .

Charles Oh, do you . . . Yes, yes . . . thanks . . .

Stephen Do you like being alive?

Charles I must say, after a certain age, the world does lose its charm.

Stephen Oh, I like being alive . . . more and more . . . despite all that . . . We'll have a good time. We'll like things. We'll dig it out . . . some hope . . .

Act Three

Morning. Breakfast in the garden. The guests have been coming in and out to eat.

Barry mending a bicycle. Julie is feeding the youngest child in the buggy. Lorraine is folding the children's clothes.

Barry (*to Julie*) . . . When a person goes away . . . when you're left . . . alone . . . you're forced to do other things . . . to find other initiatives . . . That's good, isn't it . . . from one point of view . . .

Julie (*to the child*) Good boy . . . Is that nice . . .

Barry It takes a while to see that . . . but it happens . . . I hope . . . (*Sneezes.*) I've caught a cold . . . (*to Lorraine*) I expect you'll get one.

Lorraine (*to Barry*) You're not used to coming to places like this. You should have said.

Barry (*to Lorraine*) I'm not sorry . . . you know . . . that I undressed for dinner – I can't wait to tell everyone what a lot of snobs I've seen . . .

Stephen, having woken up in the summer-house, walks across carrying a blanket.

Julie (*to Stephen*) I thought you'd gone. (*Pause.*) Have you changed your mind? Have you? Your bag's in our room.

Stephen Thank you.

Julie You know . . . Stephen . . . you know . . .

Stephen Yes . . .

Julie If . . . if . . . (*Pause.*) It's all right . . .

Stephen Sure?

Julie You . . . (*Pause.*) Nothing . . . nothing . . . (*Pause.*) What shall I say . . . when your eldest son asks for you?

   Pause.

Stephen Say . . . Say it wasn't him . . . (*He goes towards the house. Stops. To Lorraine*) You like Charles?

Lorraine He's funny.

   Stephen goes.

(*to Julie*) Coffee?

Julie Thanks.

Lorraine Julie, you haven't forgotten, I'm not coming back to London with you . . . I'm off to the seaside with the boy with the red convertible . . . He's coming to pick me up. The one you didn't like.

Julie You'll get dust up your nose . . . What does he do?

Lorraine He's a record producer. He's going to try me out in the studio.

Julie As what?

Lorraine Singer. He's encouraging – he said to me: people with less talent than you have made it. I'll be back in a couple of days . . .

Julie No longer . . .

Lorraine No . . .

Julie I will pay you more.

Lorraine Thanks.

Russell comes out.

Russell Did you read this thing about me . . .?
Unbelievable . . . Most of it's made up and I saw the edi-
tor at dinner . . . The picture's not bad . . . (*He shows it to
Julie.*)

Julie You look handsome.

Russell They've underestimated my salary by a third . . . I
don't think I ever realized how painful life could be . . .
That there's no cure for certain things.

Julie Was it a good night? Is lovely Anna coming down?

Russell She left early.

Charles She had to get back.

Julie Oh . . .

Russell She's fired, too. There's plenty of those . . . (*to
Lorraine*) Call me a cab. I let my driver go. I'm going to
Janet's and then the airport.

Julie Sorry you didn't have a better time . . .

Russell You did say Michael was coming . . .

Sophie comes on.

Barry There you are.

Sophie (*to Julie*) It's my favourite feeling – that no one
knows where I am. (*Pause.*) Do you know that?

Barry I've fixed the bike.

Sophie Why are we rushing?

Barry Don't you miss the children?

Sophie I survived a night without them.

Barry You know what I want, if someone were to ask

99

me? I want, every night, for the rest of my life, for you to sleep with me.

Sophie That's something.

Barry Isn't it?

Sophie (*to Russell*) It is still happening . . . as agreed, isn't it?

Russell Yes, yes . . . Look . . . (*He shows her the newspaper.*)

Sophie God . . . it must be awful . . . being made to look this foolish. 'His private life is something of an enigma . . .'

Russell Yes . . .

Sophie I'm sure you don't give a damn. Glad I didn't become a journalist.

Barry You are one now, aren't you?

Sophie Oh yes. (*Pause.*) I'll give my notice tomorrow . . .

Russell Good . . .

Barry Sophie . . .

Russell (*looking at the bicycles*) Are you going on those?

Sophie Yes.

Russell The scarf is lovely with your skin . . .

Sophie Thank you.

> *Stephen comes out with his bag. Charles puts his arm around Lorraine.*

Charles (*to Lorraine*) How about some fun? How people can cheer one another up . . . when they want to . . . Is it over between us already?

Lorraine For today . . .

Charles You're right . . . There's only now . . . this minute . . . this minute for ever . . . Sing something.

Lorraine Yes, why not? (*She sings to Charles in his ear.*)

Stephen (*to Russell*) I'll call you next week. We can go out . . . and discuss things . . .

Russell Yes, yes . . . Good.

Sophie kisses Julie.

Sophie Good luck . . . (*She kisses everyone. She and Barry go . . .*) See you . . . See you . . .

Charles (*to Stephen*) Your car's here, isn't it?

Stephen Yes.

Charles Are we going together?

Stephen As soon as possible. (*Pause.*) Can you . . . look the other way?

Charles (*to Lorraine*) Come and see me.

Lorraine I will, dirty face.

Stephen goes to Julie and kisses her.

Stephen Goodbye. (*He leaves.*)

Russell (*to Julie*) Next week . . . David's taking us to the Tower of London. We're not going to be tourists, don't worry. He's rented the whole place for a couple of hours. Paul'll be there –

Julie Really?

Russell If it's too early we can meet you at The Ivy . . . (*Pause. To Charles*) I liked the girl Anna . . . she was gentle . . .

Charles She wasn't beautiful enough for you . . . Any woman would welcome the chance to go out with you . . .

Russell Really?

Charles Oh yes . . . I'll send you the script tomorrow.
There's this man and this woman, trying to love another,
and another man and another woman, and they . . . go
away for the weekend together . . .

Russell . . . Back to work . . . I love it. Why does pleasure
have to be so exhausting . . .

Charles and Russell go off.
Lorraine and Julie alone.

Lorraine Julie . . . (*Pause.*) Julie . . . (*Pause.*) I'll get Joe
up. He should eat something . . .

Julie Oh yes. Good.

Lorraine And I'll run down to the village before I go.

She goes. The child starts to cry. Pause. Eventually Julie
goes to the child.

Julie Shhh . . . don't cry little man . . . Mummy loves you
. . . Daddy loves you . . . the sun is shining . . . everyone's
all right . . . don't worry . . . I'm here . . .